UNSHAKEABLE FRIEND

George Bell and the
German Churches

Edwin Robertson

CCBI
Inter-Church House
35–41 Lower Marsh
London SE1 7RL

ISBN 0 85169 234 6

Published by CCBI
Inter-Church House
35 – 41 Lower Marsh
London SE1 7RL

Typeset by Eager Typesetting Company
Printed by Delta Press

Ref CD 332

Contents

Acknowledgements

Three libraries have made this work possible and I would like to thank the staff of all three for their care and attention. They are: Lambeth Palace Library, where the 'Bell' papers are now bound into many volumes; Sion College, where the printed material is all available; the Evangelisches Archivzentral in Berlin, where much German comment is collected which never came to London or Chichester. In connection with the last of these, I am much indebted to Professor Dr. Gerhard Besier of the Kirchliche Hochschule in Zehlendorf, Berlin, and the erudite journal which he edits, "Kirchliche Zeitgeschichte" (Contemporary Church History).

I am also as usual greatly indebted to Vera Phillips for her tireless work, and to many others who have encouraged me over the years to write on this aspect of the life of George Bell, beginning with Norman Sykes and in recent years, Anthony Harvey of Westminster and Donald MacKinnon of Aberdeen.

My debts to others are evident in the text.

My gratitude must also go to those readers who recognised in this manuscript material that should be published and to Colin Davey of the CCBI, the publisher, for his careful editorial work.

Edwin Robertson

COPYRIGHT ACKNOWLEDGEMENTS

The author and publishers are grateful to Associated Press Ltd. for permission to use for the cover the Associated Press Photo of Bishop George Bell and Bishop Otto Dibelius with two Russian guards outside the Marienkirche in East Berlin on October 27th 1946.

The lines from the hymn *Christ is the King! O friends rejoice* by G. K. A. Bell (1883–1958) are reprinted on p. 160 from *Enlarged Songs of Praise 1931* by permission of Oxford University Press.

The extract on pp. 149–55 from The Official Report of the House of Lords Debate on 30th January 1958 (Hansard) is Parliamentary copyright.

Passages from Bell's letters and writings in *The Bell Papers* are reproduced by permission of Lambeth Palace Library.

Passages are reproduced:

> From Eberhard Bethge, *Dietrich Bonhoeffer*, E. T. Collins 1967; Marc Boegner, *The Long Road to Unity*, Collins 1970; Edwin Robertson, *No Rusty Swords*, Collins 1965; and Edwin Robertson, *True Patriotism*, Collins, 1973, by permission of HarperCollins Publishers.

> Excerpted from *The Bonhoeffers: Portrait of a Family* by Sabine Leibholz-Bonhoeffer copyright, 1994 Covenant Publications, 5101 N. Francisco, Chicago, Illinois, 60625, used by permission.

> From Gordon Rupp, *I seek my Brethren*, Epworth, 1975, by permission of Epworth Press.

> From G. K. A. Bell, *The Church and Humanity*, Longmans, Green & Co., 1946 and from G. K. A. Bell and Adolf Deissmann, *Mysterium Christi*, Longmans, Green & Co. 1930, by permission of Longman Group Ltd.

> From Richard Solberg, *God and Caesar in East Germany*, Macmillan New York, 1961, by permission of Macmillan (NY).

> From R. C. D. Jasper, *George Bell: Bishop of Chichester*, OUP, 1967, by permission of Oxford University Press.

> From G. K. A. Bell, *Christianity and World Order*, Penguin Books, 1940, and G. K. A. Bell, *The Kingship of Christ*, Penguin Books 1951, by permission of Penguin Books.

From Dietrich Bonhoeffer, *The Cost of Discipleship*, SCM Press 1959; Werner Hühne, *A Man to be Reckoned With*, SCM Press 1962; Klaus Scholder, *The Churches and the Third Reich*, Vol. I, SCM Press 1987, Vol. II, SCM Press 1988; W. A. Visser 't Hooft, *The First Assembly of the World Council of Churches*, SCM Press 1949, by permission of SCM Press Ltd.

From G. K. A. Bell, *Humanity and the Refugees*, University College London 1939, by permission of University College of London Press.

From Ger Van Roon, *German Resistance to Hitler*, Van Nostrand Reinhold Co. Ltd. 1971, by permission of Van Nostrand Reinhold Publishers, New York.

Prologue

In Germany, George Bell, Bishop of Chichester, was for many years the best known and most loved member of the hierarchy of the Church of England. He intended to write his life story as the main task for his retirement and divided it into three parts: The Church of England, the Ecumenical Movement and Germany. He was intimately involved with all three at an influential level; sadly he did not live to complete this work.

When he died in 1958, Norman Sykes was commissioned to write his biography. Sykes saw that the German material covered such an enormous proportion of his involvement with the world church that it was really a separate story. He therefore asked me if I would consider writing a book on the German relationship to supplement the biography. In this way, he could prevent Bell's involvement in the German situation from unbalancng the book. I had agreed to do this when Norman Sykes died. He had not really had time to do much on the biography and the task was handed to Ronald C. D. Jasper, an experienced biographer, who decided not to be hampered by earlier arrangements and saw no place for a separate volume. That, I fully understood and awaited the appearance of his biography with impatience. It was eventually published in 1967.[1] After reading Jasper's treatment of Bell I was still convinced that Norman Sykes was right. The image of "Bell" in Germany is totally different from that which could possibly appear in any English biography that did justice to a man who was also at the centre of affairs in the Church of England for so long, patron of the arts, a church statesman and spokesman for the Ecumenical Movement. To the Church of England he was one of their Bishops, who was considered by many to be a candidate for Canterbury. He had been Resident Chaplain to Archbishop Randall Davidson, whose biography he wrote. He was Dean of Canterbury at a time when religious art was ready for a renaissance. He was later Bishop of Chichester and a ready speaker in the House of Lords, sponsor of Peace movements, an influential figure at four Lambeth Conferences, an editor and writer supporting many causes which enabled the Church to take the twentieth century seriously. He saw that the Church of England was crucial in the development of the Ecumenical Movement.

All this and more is material enough for any biographer. Jasper skilfully blended the German involvement into this already crowded canvas, but there are times when it does not seem to match. There is a separate story to be told and I have tried to tell it with acknowledgements of much help from his careful work.

Ronald Jasper saw the need for this book, when in the Introduction to his biography, he emphasised that Bell's 'papers and contributions are one of the richest sources for the history of the Church in the twentieth century which this country possesses'. He adds that it is inevitable 'that one modest volume of biography fails to do it justice'. In that Introduction, he concludes, 'I hope that what I have written will provide guidance and encouragement to others in opening up the various aspects of Bell's contribution to the life of the Church in greater detail'.[2]

Notes

1. Ronald C. D. Jasper, *George Bell: Bishop of Chichester*, OUP, London, 1967.
2. *Op. cit.*, p. x.

1 Ecumenical Formation

George Kennedy Allen Bell was the son of James Bell the incumbent of the parish of Hayling Island not far from Chichester. It was there that George was born on the 4th February 1883, the first of seven children. He was educated at Westminster School and Christ Church, Oxford. He did reasonably well at Oxford and acquired a reputation as a poet. He won the Newdigate Prize for Poetry in 1904 and while still an undergraduate was the general editor of the "Golden Anthologies". After a year at Wells Theological College he was ordained in the Church of England (1907) and appointed curate at Leeds Parish Church under Samuel Bickersteth. It was at Leeds that he acquired a lasting interest in social issues. He met Albert Mansbridge, who pioneered the work of 'privileged' university students in the slum areas of Leeds, and who became a lifelong friend. Through him Bell developed an interest in the Workers' Educational Association and the University Extension Movement. After three years at Leeds he returned to Oxford as a don at Christ Church. But he carried his social concerns with him and worked extensively for "The betterment of the working class". These activities brought him into contact with William Temple and Henry Scott Holland both of whom returned to Oxford about that time. With them he worked for the University Settlements in the poorer parts of London and the north of England. During the war years and a little after, 1914–1924, he was resident chaplain to the Archbishop of Canterbury, Randall Davidson. In 1924, he was appointed Dean of Canterbury, where he sponsored a whole new awakening of the Arts. He had John Masefield's "The Coming of Christ" performed in Canterbury Cathedral – the first dramatic perform-ance in an English cathedral since the Middle Ages. After he left Canterbury he retained his interest in these performances and at his instigation T. S. Eliot wrote "Murder in the Cathedral". In 1935, when the Canterbury Festival started he played a leading role in persuading such writers as Charles Williams, Dorothy Sayers, Christopher Hassall and Christopher Fry to take part in the Festival.

In 1929, he was appointed Bishop of Chichester and, almost at once, he appointed a director of religious drama. He remained Bishop of Chichester until his retirement in 1957, a year before his death. All this was background to his leadership and formative influence upon the Ecumenical Movement and his central role in the formation of the World Council of Churches.

First Involvement with Germany

Dietrich Bonhoeffer and Bell shared the same birthday, 4th February, but separated by 23 years – 1906 and 1883.

When the Great War broke out, the old order reigned where kings went forth to war and subjects totally obeyed their call. The young Dietrich was little more than eight years old and a passionate patriot, demanding maps and pins to plot the advance of the victorious German armies. George Bell at thirty-three had no doubt that England had acted honourably in declaring war. He did, however, advise Archbishop Randall Davidson that the churches should act together in dealing with the consequences and think through the issues which would arise. He obtained permission to call a conference of Anglicans and Free churchmen – fifty in all, at Lambeth on 9th October 1914. With the help of others, he later edited a symposium, *The War and the Kingdom of God* (December 1915). Sure as he was that England was right, he knew that patriotism and victory would not solve the problems of a sinful Europe. The inevitable misery and tyranny of war could only be destroyed by the one rule of God over the world. The symposium was not even, nor were the views consistent, but Bell had started the process which would be needed once the war was over if Europe were to be one again. He saw the harm that war would do both to Britain and to Germany. He saw the Church as ineffective unless it could act as one. The Ecumenical Movement which can be said to have had its initiation in Edinburgh, 1910, fired him with enthusiasm for a World Church one day, and he never ceased to respond to a call for united action by the churches. So far he had little knowledge of Germany, except as the source of nineteenth century theology.

Adolf Deissmann

The churches in Germany, no less than in Britain, were patriotic and the Protestant theologians united to support the war effort of their Kaiser, Wilhelm II. The document of support was signed by 93 of the most distinguished theologians in Germany, led by Adolf Harnack. When Karl Barth saw the document and read the signatures he was shocked. All who had taught him theology were there supporting the Kaiser's war. From that moment he saw the bankruptcy of nineteenth century Liberal theology. Among the signatures was that of Adolf Deissmann, an established New Testament scholar whose book *Light from the Ancient East* was already a classic. It laid the foundation for the archaeological and cultural study of the background to the Bible. It was not long before Deissmann saw how destructive this war was; no longer emperors playing soldiers, but the massacre of the youth of Europe. Looking back from 1922, in the Preface to the Fourth Edition of his book, he clearly defines his change of mind:

"The cruel fate that overtook mankind in 1914 made deep inroads even on the studies to which this book is devoted. It carried off on the battlefield, or by starvation, privation and sorrow of heart, many of the scholars middle-aged as well as young who are named in the following pages, some of them, tried and trusted friends of my own, and of the survivors it also demands its tribute. Me it kept (to say nought of other things) for full seven years almost completely cut off from my old field of study. From 1914 to 1921, in such hours as were not claimed by the University, I devoted myself almost exclusively to fostering the solidarity which should prevail amongst all Protestants and throughout ecumenical Christendom, and which was most seriously endangered by the struggle of the nations."[1]

Deissmann goes on to explain the attempts he made through his Newsletter from Advent 1914 until the beginning of 1917, issuing it also in English, as the *Protestant Weekly Letter*. He lent his immense reputation as a New Testament scholar to every cause for ecumenical understanding. It was with this man that George Bell made his first and continuing contact with Germany and later it was Deissmann who introduced him to Dietrich Bonhoeffer as 'one of our best young theologians'. Bell too had lost friends, pupils and two brothers to "the cruel fate that overtook mankind in 1914". There was much in common between the two men in their experience and growing horror of war. They both moved from patriotism to something like pacifism.

The First Meeting

The International Committee of the World Alliance for Promoting International Friendship through the Churches took the bold step of calling a meeting in Holland, less than three months after the signing of the Versailles Treaty. There were representatives at it from five belligerent countries: USA, Britain, Belgium, France and Germany. There were also five neutral countries represented: Sweden, Denmark, Finland, Holland and Switzerland. It met in the Castle of Oud Wassenaar, near the Hague. The purpose was to see how the countries of Europe might work together to maintain peace. The conference was due to start on 30th September 1919, but a tense situation arose. Wilfred Monod of France refused to meet the German delegation until they publicly declared that the violation of Belgian neutrality had been morally wrong and indefensible. The Germans complained that this had not been the terms of the invitation. The Versailles Treaty had humiliated them enough by declaring them solely responsible for the war. It was Adolf Deissmann who had already in 1918 branded the infringement of Belgian neutrality as an appalling and fateful iniquity, who now solved the problem. After long consultation with French and Belgian delegates, he persuaded the German delegation, of their own accord, to affirm that the violation was an act of moral transgression. This negotiation by Deissmann made a profound impression, not least on George Bell, who had been sent by the Archbishop of Canterbury as one of the Anglican delegation to Oud Wassenaar. The other figure at this meeting to whom George Bell became closely attached was Nathan Söderblom, the Archbishop of Uppsala. Bell rated this meeting in Holland as of prime importance.

> "It was the decisive event in those early days; for it was there that the project of a World Conference of Churches on moral and social questions, under the title 'Life and Work' began to take effective shape."[2]

That World Conference would have to wait until 1925, but George Bell had seen clearly where he must go and from that moment he was committed to the Ecumenical Movement. Despite the very close affinity with Nathan Söderblom and of the Church of England to the Swedish Church he felt drawn to Germany. This was partly due to a deep sense of the injustice which was already being done to Germany in the form of punishment for the war. He talked long with Adolf Deissmann, who had not hesitated to condemn Germany's wrong. But he also learned of the hardships – 'by starvation, privation and sorrow of heart' – which Germany had suffered. Not all the wrong was on one side and victory did not mean innocence. He was to hear much the same from Dietrich Bonhoeffer in later years. It can be said that Bell learned of Europe at Oud Wassenaar from three men: Nathan Söderblom, Adolf Deissmann and Eivind Berggrav of Norway. They remained the closest friends as long as they lived.

Stockholm 1925

George Bell was Dean of Canterbury by now and had less part than he might have expected in preparing the World Conference. But he was there, one of the six hundred delegates from thirty-seven countries. The Orthodox were there in force, but the absentees were largely the Roman Catholic Church and the younger generation of Asia and Africa. "The Germans sat in a solid block by themselves, still feeling their isolation", he noted. In the end, Bell had a strong influence upon the Message of the Conference. A committee had been set up to write this Message, but it dwindled until the work was left to three men: Monod, Deissmann and

Bell. The moving spirit of the Conference was, of course, Nathan Söderblom.

> "Without him", Bell comments, "it would never have happened. It was not only his vision, but his abounding vitality, his powers of persuasion, his leadership and inspiration that made Stockholm possible".

The Conference did not shirk political issues. After the devastation of war, the churches were seeking to find their role. Their questions were: How could the Kingdom of God be recognised in the world? When they prayed, "Thy kingdom come, Thy will be done, on earth as it is in heaven", what did they look for? And did they have any part in it or did they just wait for God to act? The large themes of the conference were:

> "1. The Purpose of God for Humanity and the Duty of the Church.
> 2. The Church and Economic and Industrial problems.
> 3. The Church and Social and Moral problems.
> 4. The Church and International Relations.
> 5. The Church and Christian Education.
> 6. Methods of cooperative and federative action by the Christian Communities."[3]

Looking back a quarter of a century later, Maurice Villain describes the Stockholm Conference as ambiguous in its theology. He particularly criticises Wilfrid Monod for his inadequate and misleading interpretation of the Church and the Kingdom of God. As he described Monod's view, it was that the Church had a direct responsibility and duty to undertake 'the completion of the creation, the humanising of humanity, the establishment on one globe of a family in which the Son of Man would be the first among many brethren'. Villain could not see this as a true description of the 'building up of the Body of Christ, the Kingdom of God on earth'. Bell noted the same weakness and it was the germ of an idea for theological discussion in which he and Deissmann would play leading roles.[4]

The strength of this Conference however was brought out clearly by George Bell in the Official Report which he wrote and published in the following year.[5]

All those who watched George Bell at work in these ecumenical meetings, committees and drafting sessions remarked upon his silent note-taking. The exuberance of Nathan Söderblom, whose pragmatism brushed aside all theological difficulties as already solved, was admired but not shared by Bell. He was the honey-bee Söderblom said who absorbed all the riches of the conversations and speeches but remained the "silent bell, which never rang unnecessarily". Bell would have agreed with Maurice Villain's comment that "it was impossible to define the Church's views on these problems so long as there was any ambiguity about the essential nature of the Church itself".[6] For this reason he made clear in his Continuation Committee that Life and Work needed a theological undergirding. For this he turned to the Germans.

The Follow-Up

Bell attempted to establish a Church of England Council on Foreign Relations, but it was delayed so long that it lost its drive and from Bell's point of view fell into the wrong hands. He also attempted to gather small groups of teachers and theologians from different churches to think through their theological difficulties and the problems which Söderblom had too quickly disposed of. In this he had the wise guidance of Adolf Deissmann. The most effective work which Bell and Deissmann did together was the calling of the Anglo-German Theological Conferences which are dealt with in detail in the next chapter. There were three of these, held successively in Canterbury, Eisenach and Chichester, between April 1927 and March 1931. It was the last of these conferences which established beyond doubt the need for a theological undergirding of the Ecumenical Movement, and in particular that practical part which sought to move the churches to united action, the Life and Work movement. Although the other side of the Ecumenical Movement had theology enough in its discussion of the Faith and Order of the churches, Life and Work needed much clearer theological thinking. The conferences had secured a place among certain circles in Germany for George Bell. He was immensely respected and trusted by these theologians in Germany who realised already that something was threatening in their country which would challenge, if not destroy, the Church. Of course, Bell was concerned with more than the German churches. He took a leading part in the Continuation Committee after Stockholm and as Bishop of Chichester in 1929, proposed a comprehensive resolution, supporting the Kellog-Briand Pact which had condemned recourse to war for the solution of international disputes, and further defining the role of the churches in the peace movement:

> "We believe that war, considered as an institution for the settlement of international disputes, is incompatible with the mind and method of Christ, and therefore incompatible with the mind and method of his Church".[7]

Typically he was not content to leave his resolution stating mere generalities or even worthy principles. He spelt out what that meant and called upon all Christian Communions to "declare in unmistakable terms that they will not countenance any war or encourage their countrymen to serve in any war, with regard to which the government of their country has refused an offer to submit the dispute to arbitration". The World Alliance accepted this proposal and gave it much publicity. It stimulated in England the ecumenically based 'Christ and Peace' movement which Bell chaired for more than a year as it brought the issue to the fore. If the nations could approve of the Kellog-Briand Pact they should act upon their words. In 1930, he persuaded the Lambeth Conference to give support to this principle.

In the World Alliance Bell now played a dominant role, drafting the Constitution which made it possible for it to function. That was accepted in September 1930.

Notes

1. Adolf Deissmann, *Light from the Ancient East*, Fourth Edition, Harper and Brothers, New York and London, 1922, p. ix.
2. G. K. A. Bell, *The Kingship of Christ*, Penguin Books, London, 1954, p. 26.
3. G. K. A. Bell, *The Stockholm Conference, 1925*, OUP, 1926, p. 2.
4. Maurice Villain, *Unity*, Harvill Press, London, 1963, p. 32n[3].
5. G. K. A. Bell, *The Stockholm Conference, 1925, The Official Report of the Universal Christian Conference on Life and Work, 19th–30th August 1925*, OUP, 1926.
6. Maurice Villain *op. cit.*, p. 32.
7. *The Bell Papers* in Lambeth Palace Library, Vol. I f. 21 Continuation Committee Minutes, Eisenach, 1929. *Times* article, 16th September 1929 (cutting in *The Bell Papers*).

2   The Relation of the Kingdom of God to Human Society

On 29th August 1925 at the Stockholm World Conference of the Churches, the Very Reverend G. K. A. Bell, Dean of Canterbury, expressed the hope that some time in the future a group of representatives of different countries might meet together for some common intellectual task under the shadow of his cathedral. He consulted with Dr. Adolf Deissmann, Chairman of the Stockholm Theological Commission and together his hope was realised in April 1927, albeit only between two countries – Britain and Germany. For the duration of one week thirteen British and German theologians worked at a "common intellectual task", which had been the principal concern of the Stockholm meetings, "the nature of the Kingdom of God and its relation to human society".

A Theological Responsibility

This intensive contact of British and German theologians reading papers and discussing at length their different solutions to the question of relevance, sharing the different experiences they had had during a war, seen from different sides, was in itself a worthwhile operation. It certainly cemented Bell's relationship with Germany, which was to be so fruitful in both countries. Bell also had a very clear idea of what he thought was the responsibility of the theologians to the 'front line troops' of the churches, the parish priests and pastors.

When two of these conferences were reported with contributions from the participants in *Mysterium Christi* in 1930, he included a final paper on "The Church and the Theologian". In that paper he argued that the Church had a duty to the theologian, but also that the theologian had a special duty to the Church. He saw this from two points of view.

> "On the one hand, he (the theologian) ought to seek for some personal contact with the parish priest or pastor and the tasks in which he is daily engaged. He must not dwell altogether apart from the turmoil of the market place, or regard its problems or the work of the clergy ministering in that turmoil as no concern of his. And besides this, the theologian ought to take the world of man into his purview from the strictly scientific point of view; the thoughts, feelings and activities of men to whom God comes and who enjoy, or may enjoy, a

religious experience, form a part (however small a part) of his material. The theologian has, as it were, to organise all his material and relate each of the many parts to the rest. And as the theologian is a man who communicates his results to men it is necessary that he be alive to other men's thoughts and affairs. Indeed, in some branches of theology, where the theologian is in a special degree the interpreter of the religious experience of human beings, he may have the same sort of relation to that experience as the musician who sets his songs to music has to the poet who makes these songs. He may not only follow the words, understanding them and realising them as well as he can, but he may also express what he feels about them as a theologian and add a new force and fire to those words – the religious experience of human beings."[1]

In this way George Bell argued for a human kinship with the pastor. He also added a warning that the theologian must learn patience. He puts truth above all things, but it is not for him to parade his new insights without regard to the harm they might do. The private discussions of the senior common room need not be the headlines of the press – not even the church press.

> "Personal opinion is one thing, but teaching in the name of the Church is another; and it is a distinction to be observed by all."[2]

What is more important to our understanding of George Bell's unique relationship to Germany is that he saw as early as the 'twenties the danger of theological isolation. Karl Barth had recognised this in 1914 when he read the list of those who signed to support the Kaiser's war. They were certainly out of touch then with the parishes. In the problems raised by that war, theology did little to help the work of the pastors. England was perhaps a little better, but not much. In the crisis theology failed.

Perhaps this was why Deissmann insisted that the German theologians at the Canterbury Conference in 1927 should all be young.

Deissmann's Letter

Adolf Deissmann did not come to Canterbury, but he sent a letter pointing out the importance of the theme "the nature of the Kingdom of God and its relation to human society". He rejected the view that there was an irreconcilable difference between the Anglo-Saxon and German views of the Kingdom of God, "rather that the many-sided character of the Kingdom of God is united in the various Christian churches in a parallelogram of ecumenical powers".[3] He then at once raised the question which occupied him and George Bell for the rest of their lives. "To what extent does the Dominion of God influence the affairs of this age?" He quoted from C. F. Mayer's *The Saint*, which is about St. Thomas of Canterbury and the King:

> 'To whom do you appeal Thomas?', laughed the King, 'to the Holy Trinity?'
> 'I appeal to the Gospels', whispered Thomas, 'which are the record of Him in whom there was found no unrighteousness.'
> 'These are the words of no true Bishop', cried the King in noble disgust. 'These are the words of a wretched heretic! The sacred Book of the Gospels belongs to a pearl-embroidered altar hanging, and has nothing to do with the order of the world or with things as they really are!'[4]

The Swiss poet, said Deissmann, had formulated the problem in the classical manner and he put himself with Thomas and not the King.

Other-Worldly and This-Worldly

At the first Anglo-German theological conference, there was determination not to lose the transcendent dimension of the kingdom of God, nor to identify it too closely with the Church. Sir Edwin Hoskyns was unequivocal:

> "The eschatological imagery was fundamental to primitive Christianity because it adequately guarded and preserved the other-worldly character of God, of the Church and of Christian morality."[5]

C. H. Dodd, was already developing his realised eschatology:

> "Instead of the abrupt contrast between this age and the next – we have the idea of a progressive revelation of the kingdom of God within this historical order. The process however is not finished within this order."[6]

All this Bell must have heard many times. The Germans also had their professional theological debates. But it was from them that he learned of the conditions in Germany where the attractions of National Socialism, as early as 1927, were growing. Stählin of Münster was close to the youth of Germany:

> "After a period in which earthly standards of life were regarded, with a naïve matter-of-factness, as the goal of our ambitions, German youth of today is experiencing a passionate longing for forms of community life in which is found an ultimate aim and

an ultimate obligation. The question of the German youth movement is the question of the kingdom of God. Thus it is of decisive importance whether the kingdom of God is to be regarded as in absolute opposition to all forms of earthly life, or whether the nature of the kingdom of God will be learned through the symbols of any particular form of human association. And it is not a matter of indifference whether the secret of sexual love or the life of the nation or the state will be felt as the symbol of the secrets of the kingdom of God. The seriousness with which the state and its ordinances are regarded prevents the individualistic, mystical or sentimental misunderstanding of the kingdom of God."[7]

Wilhelm Stählin was a very important member of the team of German theologians and he made a great impression on Bell. They were about the same age and shared some experience of pastoral work as well as involvement with student work in the university. Bell had learned a great deal from his three years pastoral work as a curate in Leeds, and his brief period as a don in Oxford had given him experience of working with students.

Stählin had been pastor of St. Lorenz in Nuremberg and was by now Professor of Theology at Münster. In contrast, Bell always claimed that he was himself no theologian, but he asked theological questions, particularly in the area of church-state relations. His time as chaplain to Randall Davidson and his experience of the 1928 Prayer Book debate brought him again into the field of church-state relations. The issue of the Prayer Book greatly interested the Germans, but that was after the Canterbury Conference. Bell's pastoral concerns led him to listen carefully to Stählin because of his considerable association with the Youth Movement in Germany. He also warmed to Stählin's direct approach:

"Any Christian who evades active responsibility for the organisations of earthly life makes the kingdom of God either a purely inward thing or something wholly invisible and other-worldly, or else a hope for the future which is beyond all earthly realisation. In this way God's claim to sovereignty over this world is denied, and the organisations of human life given over to demonic powers. This is shown just as clearly in the relations of the sexes and in national associations as in the large contexts of our academic and political life".[8]

The *Völkisch* Movement

For those who were listening to Wilhelm Stählin – and Bell was the best listener I have ever known – whether in his paper or in the many informal discussions between sessions, a new light was being thrown on the situation in Germany. If the horrors of Nazism took us by surprise a decade later, it was because we had not listened. Bell listened. What Stählin was saying about Germany concerned the youth who would later fall completely under Hitler's spell.

The *völkisch* movement about which Stählin spoke was based upon a strong sense of being a people, with an identity and pride in their culture. It usually meant an awareness of being a people with a purpose in history. Klaus Scholder explains its importance for the rise of Nazism:

> "The development of the so-called *völkisch* movement or *völkisch* idea must be seen as one of the most important things to happen in the period during and after the First World War. Without it the spread of National Socialism is inconceivable, in fact the NSDAP [The National Socialist German Workers Party] was simply a *völkisch* movement which became a political party in the sense that the Communist parties are Marxism embodied in political parties."[9]

It was the understanding of this that enabled Bell to recognise the nature of Nazism long before the other church leaders began to take it seriously as a threat to European civilisation. He could have had no better informant in the 'twenties than Wilhelm Stählin.

Many welcomed the *völkisch* movement because it seemed to give purpose and hope to the young people of Germany; others feared its pagan potential; but Stählin showed that one could welcome it in principle, but remain critical of certain elements in it. In 1924, when he was still a pastor in Nuremburg, he responded favourably to a movement that he thought could be introduced into the youth work of the church. He did this with eyes wide open to its dangers. He gave a lecture on it which was subsequently published. In that lecture he explored positively what was legitimate in the *völkisch* movement, showing that he understood its appeal to young Germans who had been ashamed of their country. They wanted to be proud of being German and not handicapped by the guilt of a war initiated by an earlier generation. Stählin admitted this and was therefore far more credible when he came to criticise the movement. He recognised its three main aspects – 'the experience of the *Volk*', the 'consciousness of solidarity among the members of the *Volk*', and the 'will to act'. He saw the value in this movement because it made clear 'to our rootless and high-handed contemporaries, trapped in the cult of person-ality or the class struggle, that they were bound to a particular place in the world and their lives to a particular hour of history'.[10]

He also welcomed the new relationship to the neighbour – namely solidarity. And the will to act seemed good to him, because passionate action for a lofty goal had its own value even when 'quiet rationality and clarity of purpose' were lacking. But he saw how easily this could be exploited and he detected already serious weaknesses: the danger of a loss of inwardness when a national activity became an end in itself; the attempt to forget one's own guilt and to reach out for quick and comfortable solutions; and, finally, the flight into anti-semitism, which he called a 'gigantic blunder' and 'a shameful sign of lack of insight and decency'. His lecture sounds nationalistic today, but we need to remember that at that time, German Protestantism had not yet worked out its relationship to this prevalent *völkisch* movement. There were those who welcomed its national aspirations, approved its affirmation of law and order, and were ready to join in the struggle against Marxism and 'Mammonism'. Those same people who saw hope in the movement were also repelled by its raucous anti-semitism, the style of its political campaigning and most certainly resisted its religious claims. This was where Stählin was most helpful. He saw clearly and increasingly that there was a danger in the movement if it were given any religious connotation. When Stählin, who had responded positively to the new hope that youth found in the movement, spoke to a group of pastors in Thuringia in 1924, the critical side was predominant. He insisted that it would be good if there were pastors in the *völkisch* movement so long as a criticism of all movements 'governed by Christianity' was not lost.

By 1927, Stählin was a great deal more critical of the *völkisch* movement and saw more clearly its dangers. He was troubled when he came to Canterbury. That is clear from his paper and was, no doubt, clearer to the sensitive George Bell in his discussions with him.

German Patriotism

Paul Althaus who was also at Canterbury in 1927 was quite different. His paper on 'The Kingdom of God and the Church' made no reference to any such tension. Yet, that summer, he spoke at the Königsberg *Kirchentag* (a Protestant Church Congress) which passed what was called 'The Patriotic Declaration' showing that the *völkisch* issue had moved from the periphery of the Church to the centre. The older members at the *Kirchentag* accepted it as a 'Fatherland *Kirchentag*' – good, old-fashioned patriotism, which never did anyone any harm. But this was not so for the young Paul Althaus. In carefully marked formulations he developed the fundamentals of a new political theology, which made possible the full cooperation of the Protestant churches with, first the *völkisch* movement, and later, Nazism. The majority of those who heard him at the 1927 *Kirchentag* were under the impression that it was just a new version of the old nationalist and conservative theology. But reading it now, it is easy to see in which direction he was going. No doubt that is due to hindsight, but even at the time, Karl Barth was suspicious.

> "I find in this lecture everything that impresses me about you and it is at the same time ominous; your capacity to be open on all sides and to be carried away by your enthusiasm which, from my point of view, is also the capacity to swallow and approve entirely too much for me to be able always to hear the totally clear sound of your own trumpet."[11]

Bell must very soon have recognised how right Deissmann was to insist on *young* German theologians. These two, Wilhelm Stählin and Paul Althaus, could hardly have been better chosen if the purpose had been to inform British theologians of what was really going on in Germany. There is no indication of this German patriotism in the paper Paul Althaus presented to the Canterbury Conference or in his essay in *Mysterium Christi*. The essay in *Mysterium Christi*, is a purely academic and quite brilliant essay on theories of the Atonement. The paper presented at Canterbury may hide some ideas in the way that Barth indicated in his comment on the *Kirchentag* lecture, but they are difficult to find, and he almost sounds, at the end of his paper, like the later Bonhoeffer.

> "The church does her service to the life of Civilisation, and to world organisations chiefly *indirectly* – that, out of her, men of lively conscience and eschatological seriousness go into all professions and offices, but also *directly* and publicly through criticism by her responsible speakers of the state and administration of social and international life. That the Church, which truly is and remains also a piece of the world, directs this criticism equally against herself is a proof of its earnestness!"[12]

Only a few months later, in the Kirchentag lecture, he was facing two questions about the *völkisch* movement: "Is there a path that leads from the *völkisch* purpose to the Church?" and "What is the path from the Church to the realm of the *Volk?*" It is very unlikely that with Stählin present they did not discuss the first question at Canterbury. For Althaus, like Stählin, condemned all approaches to a *volkisch* religion. The whole *völkisch* movement he argued must not be allowed to find itself in a *völkisch* religion, but in the Church's Christian Gospel. That sounds satisfactory, because the destination of the *völkisch* movement becomes the Church, but there is a second question which concerns the movement of the Church towards the *Volk*. Althaus went on to deduce that the Church must become a *Volkskirche* (a church of the people), which he interpreted

14

as a Church of *the Volk,* as *Volk,* as a totality of life. Serving the *Volk* would mean, given the presuppositions of the *völkisch* movement, proclaiming a truly German version of the Gospel. It would mean the Church entering into the organic life and living customs of the *Volk.* Nothing less than Germany's destiny is involved in this. It was in this way that Althaus managed to give theological legitimacy to National Socialism. [13]

Stählin was not at the second Anglo-German Theological Conference in Eisenach, but George Bell saw that he was needed to help them understand what Althaus was really saying. By the third conference Stählin was back and it was Althaus who did not come to Chichester in 1929. By then, he was more concerned with Germany's destiny than with ecumenical discussion. These three conferences were crucial for Bell's understanding of the movement that led to National Socialism and the dilemma of the Protestant Churches in seeking to be central in the fulfilment of Germany's destiny.

Faith and Order: Lausanne, 1927

While the Life and Work Movement was gaining its strength, the earlier parallel movement known as Faith and Order was lively and active. Many leading churchmen took part in both movements. Deissmann was Chairman of the Continuation Committee of Life and Work, and also one of the four vice-chairmen of the Faith and Order Conference which met in Lausanne in 1927. On the first full day of that Conference, Thursday 4th August, he delivered a powerful address on "The Church's Message to the World: the Gospel". He reminded the Conference that only the English language carried an acceptable translation of the Greek "*Euaggelion*" – "The possession of the word 'gospel' is one of the greatest spiritual treasures that are entrusted to English-speaking Christendom", he said. [14] He argued for the unity of the Church – not a uniformity, but through speaking one word to the world. He knew that the Church in its unity had power. In this power it is called upon to preach – "O Zion, that bringest *good tidings,* get thee up into a high mountain". It is called to "lift up its voice with strength" and to proclaim to the world, "Behold your God".

Something of his power as a preacher comes over as he develops that theme.

> "So long as the Church preaches the Gospel from the narrow valleys and deep abysses of mutual suspicion and isolation, her message does not penetrate to the world; it dies away piteously on the hard rocky walls, it fades away in the shadow and cold

mists of the valley bottoms. But if the united Churches together mount, as the Zion of today, to the topmost heights of the holy mountain, and call aloud from there to the world as ambassadors on behalf of Christ "Repent ye, for the Kingdom of God is at hand", "Be ye reconciled to God", then indeed that Gospel which in the age of the Roman Caesars gave a new direction to men's lives and even to the Mediterranean world as a whole, will do today for a world grown vaster, that for which, in the misery of its pride and bestiality, of its hatred, its guilt and its perplexity, it is hungry and athirst."[14]

Although George Bell was not at the conference in Lausanne, he followed the events and read the reports carefully. In particular, he welcomed the first two Section Reports: 'The Call to Unity', adopted unanimously by the Conference, and 'The Church's Message to the World – the Gospel', which it received for transmission to the churches.[15]

This report, so strongly influenced by Deissmann, was of great importance to Bell. He included it in the second series of his *Documents on Christian Unity* and it survived in his *A Selection from the First and Second Series: 1920–1930*, which appeared many years later. The original *Documents on Christian Unity, Second Series* was made available for Bishops at the Lambeth Conference in 1930, in which Bell acted as episcopal secretary.

The following paragraph from the "Message" is enough to show why Bell was so pleased with its acceptance.

"The Gospel is the sure source of power for social regeneration. It proclaims the only way by which humanity can escape from those class and race hatreds which devastate society at present into the enjoyment of national well-being and international friendship and peace. It is also a gracious invitation to the non-Christian world, East and West, to enter into the joy of the living Lord.

Sympathising with the anguish of our generation, with its longing for intellectual sincerity, social justice and spiritual inspiration, the Church in the eternal Gospel meets the needs and fulfils the God-given aspirations of the modern world."[16]

In September 1927, Bell was in Marburg for two weeks. There is no clear indication of what he was doing there, except an enigmatic entry reading: "I was occupied peacefully and all day, partly with lessons and partly with meetings and hospitality". It sounds as though he was making an attempt to learn German which he never mastered! Of course, there were many other good reasons for being in Marburg when he was cementing relations between British and German theologians.

The German interest in the fate of the English Prayer Book

In 1927 and 1928, the Germans watched a strange controversy in England concerning the Book of Common Prayer. It should have been a simple matter to revise it and, although there would be dissenting and conservative voices, surely it was not beyond the wit of the Church of England to bring its 17th century Prayer Book up to date. But those who thought so reckoned without the strange character of the Establishment in England. The Anglo-Catholics were in the ascendance during the 'twenties and they took a large part in the revision of the Book of Common Prayer. It was not Bell's major interest but he had to explain to his new-found German friends the extraordinary drama that was staged in England over the revision. The controversy was understood. There are high-church Lutherans too. It was also easy to explain that it had to be passed by the Church Assembly, and that was by overwhelming majorities: 34 to 4 in the House of Bishops; 253 to 37 in that of the clergy; 230 to 92 in that of the laity. Archbishop Davidson was luke-warm in his support, but he was advised of its necessity. The change could not be made without the consent of Parliament. With such majorities in the Church Assembly it should have been self-evident that it would pass through Parliament. That did not, however, prove to be the case. The two principal lay Evangelical opponents were Joynson-Hicks, the Home Secretary, and Inskip, the Solicitor General. Both of these were members of the Church Assembly and had been defeated there. They carried their battle with more effect into the House of Commons. The new Prayer Book was thought to be a sell-out to Anglo-Catholics and to Rome.

This fear was accentuated by the conversations being conducted at that time between Cardinal Mercier and Lord Halifax and others about common points of faith between Anglo-Catholics and Roman Catholics. The conversations had no immediate results, but they revived pan-Protestant fears of Rome.

The House of Lords discussed the Bill for the revision of the Book of Common Prayer with commendable care. Adrian Hastings summarises the debate in the Lords with approval:

> "The Bill passed the Lords, where the three day debate (12th to 14th December 1927) provided a splendid expression of the Established Church, laymen and bishops, discussing the pros and cons of liturgical change with great maturity. The debate itself almost justified Establishment."[17]

This was not true of the Commons. The discussion was short, full of abuse and irrelevancies and resulted in the Bill being defeated twice, in December 1927 and January 1928.

Bell was Dean of Canterbury at this time and firmly in favour of the Establishment. After the first defeat in the Commons he wrote to the Bishop of Jarrow "we shall both be on the same non-disestablishment platform if the cry is being raised in the summer".

The Germans watched with great interest what the Church of England would do. The separation of church and state in the Weimar Republic had made them sensitive to changes in this relationship. They had found no satisfactory solution. They had been orphaned after the abdication of the Kaiser and it proved impossible to find a substitute for the once strong links between 'throne and altar'. Some watched England with sympathy, others proffered radical advice. No secular body should dictate to the Church the terms of its worship. Disestablishment was the only answer. Others recognising England's embarrassment offered only sympathy. Adolf Deissmann wrote to Bell twice during the critical period:

> "9th January 1928: It was with the greatest interest and the deepest sympathy that I followed these serious events in the recent Church history of your country."

> "12th July: Now I wish to say a word of sympathy in connection with the hard experience you have had in your Church life. I am very anxious to hear at Eisenach your opinion."

There is little doubt that the subject occupied many an hour in Eisenach and that others beside Deissmann were anxious to hear Bell's opinion. They did not have long to wait. In the following year, 1929, he published A Brief Sketch of the Church of England. The small book did much to help the Germans understand the dilemma of the Church of England. By this time Bell was Bishop of Chichester and it was for him a matter of discipline whether his churches should be encouraged or even allowed to use the Book that had failed to receive parliamentary consent. He traced the problem to the report issued by the Royal Commission on Ecclesiastical Discipline in 1906, which had recommended Convocation to prepare proposals for the revision of the Prayer Book, 'with a view to their enactment by parliament'.

The problem passed. The bishops allowed or encouraged the use of the 1928 Prayer Book, according to their persuasion, and the Protestant protests became weaker with time. But Bell came closest to his German friends in the experience of this time and his book helped them to understand the unique character of the Church of England. His own views were not very strongly in favour of the Prayer Book but he believed that the Church should legislate on its own liturgy:

> "It is permissible to enquire whether it may not still be possible, in accordance with the old theory, if the Church remains established, for Convocation to legislate as effectively and finally, subject only to the Royal Assent, on spiritual matters as Parliament legislates on temporal matters."[18]

The importance of this controversy for the relationship between George Bell and Germany lies in the events which were to follow in a few years in Germany. For then Bell would be one of the very few British churchmen who understood the much more fatal issue of church and state which would confront the German churches.

The Lambeth Conference of 1930

Most bishops of the Church of England will attend a Lambeth Conference during their time, a number will attend two and a few even three; but George Bell had the distinction of being present at four Lambeth Conferences over a period of thirty-eight years. All four found him pushing the cause of unity and peace. The four Conferences were in 1920, 1930, 1948 and 1958. He was not, of course, a bishop in 1920 but as resident chaplain to the Archbishop he was assistant secretary to the conference. As such he was already quite influential. When Archbishop Cosmo Lang of York, who chaired the 1920 Lambeth Conference's Committee on Reunion, conceived the idea of an "Appeal to all Christian People", rather than only to the Church of England, it was Bell who proposed the setting up of a small committee of younger bishops to draft it and he himself acted as their secretary. That appeal is the first document selected for his *Documents on Christian Unity*. It calls for a common fellowship, a common ministry, and a common service to the world. It concludes:

> "We place this ideal first and foremost before ourselves and our own people. We call upon them to make the effort to meet the demands of a new age with a new outlook. To all other Christian people whom our words may reach we make the same appeal. We do not ask that any one Communion should consent to be absorbed into another. We do ask that all should unite in a new and great endeavour to recover and to manifest in the world the unity of the Body of Christ for which he prayed."[19]

The Lambeth Conference of 1930 which Bell attended as Bishop of Chichester was the main reason for the postponement of the third Anglo-German Theological Conference until March 1931.

To the minds of some, particularly the younger bishops, it was a Lambeth Conference of very little importance. Larger national issues overshadowed it. On 24th October 1929, the New York Stock Market had collapsed and set in motion an economic depression throughout the world. By the time the Lambeth Conference met in July–August 1930, the number of unemployed in Britain had risen to the unprecedented height of more than two million. The Labour government tottered and eventually fell. It was replaced in August 1931 by a coalition government. During this economic blizzard, the Lambeth Conference seemed almost irrelevant. Bell, as the episcopal secretary, did his work thoroughly and pressed his concern for peace and unity. But the Church of England looked surprisingly Victorian in 1930; the Archbishop was Cosmo Lang, a Victorian indeed, who provided little or no leadership for the Church of England. He was flanked by Winnington-Ingram (London), Headlam (Gloucester) and Henson (Durham) all of whom had made their mark before the death of Queen Victoria. It was easy to be depressed as the Church of England lost support in the nation. There was a revival of a kind in the public schools, but the people generally were turning to the left as the elections of the 'twenties had shown. If they went to church at all it was to the Methodists, whose Union had added new vigour to that denomination. However, there were younger bishops with left-wing tendencies and a determination to come to grips with the social issues of the day. Adrian Hastings numbers among these younger bishops George Bell, Kenneth Kirk later of Oxford, Cyril Garbett at Southwark, later Winchester and York, but pre-eminently William Temple, who moved from Manchester to York, 1929, at the height of his powers and aged only forty-seven. Bell sensed a kind of revival and was part of it.

There is a letter by Bishop Herbert Hensley Henson, written during the Lambeth Conference of 1930, which sums up the confusion of the older bishops with the issues of the new age. It is written to a younger clergyman, describing his surprise at the frankness of a young married woman whom he had met at dinner the night before in London. She had advocated the propriety of unmarried women taking lovers now that birth control was available. He was startled and mentioned that the Bishops at Lambeth were going to discuss birth control. She replied that "the use of contraceptives was universal in her class and she could not understand how there could be any question as to its rightness". Henson comments:

> "I was much interested and not a little surprised at her
> confidence, lack of reticence, and complete detachment from
> conventional sex-morality. I realised that I belong to a past
> generation and am probably 'walking in a darkness that may be

felt' when I try to understand the problems of the hour. I shall be glad when I can shake off the dust from my feet against this Babylon, and get back to Auckland."[20]

Bell accomplished quite a lot but it was a dull Lambeth. That same year, 1930, saw the 400th anniversary of the Augsburg Confession. The celebrations were important for Protestant Germany and should have been for the Church of England, whose Thirty-Nine Articles are derived from it. But it was thought to be too controversial as had been the celebrations of the 500th anniversary of the Reformation to Randall Davidson in 1917 and it was almost ignored in England. Bell sent his Dean of Chichester, the Very Rev. A. S. Duncan-Jones as an observer to the Augsburg Celebrations and thus quickened in him a lifelong interest in the German churches.

The Third Anglo-German Theological Conference

George Bell invited the participants to Chichester this time, in March 1931. England was still in the throes of a financial crisis. Germany was worse and Nazism was rampant in the German churches. It was the year that Bonhoeffer went to the Cambridge Conference of the World Alliance, for which a preparatory conference was held in Hamburg to define the German position. Althaus published a statement with Emanuel Hirsch saying that "there can be no understanding between us Germans and the nations that were victorious in the World War".

The Anglo-German Conference took as its theme at Chichester 'Corpus Christi'. The papers prepared for that conference were again printed in Theology. Reading through the papers now it is not difficult to detect the influence of what was happening in Germany.

The results of the 'Reichstag Election' in September 1930 had been spectacular. Most people expected the Nazis to gain ground, but it was a landslide. In a little over two years the NSDAP had raised its votes from 2.6% to 18.3%, and its seats in the Reichstag from 12 to 107. When the results are carefully examined, it can be seen that the larger gains were made in the predominantly Protestant areas.

This is partially explained by the fact that Protestants had no specifically Protestant Party. The Catholics had, the Centre Party (Centrum), which attracted a high proportion of votes in Catholic areas. This explanation is supported by the fact that the Socialists also polled a higher proportion of the votes in Protestant areas. But there is more to say. The Protestants had lost faith in the old system, giving declining support to the Weimar Republic. At this point they were lost and in need of a cause. Theology in Germany had long been isolationist, conducted among theologians and having little effect on the life of the Church. A strong and relevant Protestant theology might have helped them to find their way in the baffling political scene.

Things were changing, however, and a public debate occurred in Berlin when Karl Barth lectured in January 1931 to a massive and lively audience and was refuted by Otto Dibelius eight days later. Shortly afterwards, General Superintendent Dibelius came to England to attend the Anglo-German Theological Conference in Chichester and to share the chairmanship of that conference with Bishop Bell. The issue in the Berlin debate was not a confrontation between theory and practice, as Dibelius had insisted, but about the need for a radical re-examination of the very foundations of the Church. This was happening as young men were coming into the leadership of the Protestant Church. There was no better example of this than the young German pastor, Hermann Sasse, who attended the second and third of the Anglo-German Theological Conferences, at Eisenach and Chichester. Sasse's comments on the state of German theology were that "a fatal chasm has opened up between theology and the practical work of the churches" and "the substantial work of re-building the church and the profound theological work of the last decade stand side by side with virtually no connection between them".

At Chichester Hermann Sasse read his paper on "The Nature of the Institutional Expression of the Idea" [of the Church as the Body of Christ].[21] He did not bring the Berlin controversy into the theological conference explicitly, but both he and Dibelius knew what both had said. He did, however, begin to work out the meaning of the statement, unique to Christianity, that a community of believers could be designated as 'the body of Christ'.

Notes

1. *Mysterium Christi*, edited by G. K. A. Bell and Adolf Deissmann, Longmans, Green & Co., London, 1930, p. 283.
2. *Ibid.*, p. 284.
3. *Theology*, SPCK, London, Vol. XIV (Jan–June 1927), p. 284.
4. *Ibid.*, p. 285.
5. *Ibid.*, p. 255 (the full text, pp. 249–255).
6. *Ibid.*, p. 260 (the full text, pp. 259–260).
7. *Ibid.*, p. 295 (the full text, pp. 293–295).
8. *Ibid.*, p. 294.
9. Klaus Scholder, *The Churches and the Third Reich*, Vol. 1, SCM Press, London, 1987, p. 74.
10. *Ibid.*, p. 110 (German text, Wilhelm Stählin, *Via Vitae: Lebenserinnerungen*, Kassel, 1966, pp. 176–191).
11. *Ibid.*, p. 112 (from letter dated, 19th September 1927).
12. *Theology*, Vol. XIV, p. 292.

13. Klaus Scholder, *op. cit.*, Vol. 1, pp. 111–113.
14. *Faith and Order: Lausanne 1927*, edited H. N. Bate, SCM Press, London 1927, p. 46.
15. *Ibid.*, pp. 460–463.
16. *Ibid.*, pp. 462–463.
17. Adrian Hastings, *A History of English Christianity 1920–1985*, Collins, London, 1986, pp. 205–206.
18. G. K. A. Bell, *A Brief Sketch of the Church of England*, SCM Press, London, 1929, p. 124.
19. *Documents on Christian Unity – 1920–24*, edited G. K. A. Bell, OUP, 1924, p. 5.
20. *More Letters from Herbert Hensley Henson*, edited E. F. Braley, SPCK, London, 1954, pp. 62–63.
21. *Theology*, Vol. XXII, pp. 318–323.

3 George Bell and Dietrich Bonhoeffer

The first meeting with George Bell was for most people a memorable occasion. It was quite different from listening to him speak at some public meeting or even talking at a reception. Bell's meetings were deliberate, often contrived, but even when accidental, they had a kind of purpose about them. He inspired total confidence.

Dietrich Bonhoeffer must have had that feeling at Novi Sad in Yugoslavia. His first acquaintance with Bell had been at second hand, when Siegmund-Schultze asked him to translate "A Brief Sketch of the Church of England".[1] His biographer Bethge assures us that all he did was to check the translation of a friend, but it was a slight connection. The name was known. Their first meeting took place in the tumultuous days of 1933 when Bonhoeffer hardly left Berlin. He refused all invitations to conferences except one – the World Alliance conference at Sofia, 15th–30th September 1933.

The World Alliance and the Life and Work conferences usually took place in close conjunction – roughly the same time and at places not too far from each other. The Life and Work conference was held at Novi Sad. The German representatives to these two conferences were very different: at Sofia, Bonhoeffer in full throttle against the 'German Christians', as they were called because of their insistence on the German character of the Evangelical Church in Germany; at Novi Sad, Theodor Heckel, the foreign affairs minister of the official Church. The Life and Work conference met 9th–12th September and took some firm decisions, expressing concern about the situation in Germany. Those due to attend the meetings of the World Alliance were forewarned of this and a small delegation, including Bonhoeffer, came to Novi Sad on 13th September before their conference started. It was then that Bonhoeffer met Bell for the first time.

Theodor Heckel

It is extremely difficult to assess Theodor Heckel. He began on the side of the angels and never completely went over to the 'German Christians' who would have tied the Church to the Nazi State, but he compromised and Bonhoeffer never forgave him. Eberhard Bethge sums him up:

> "As the foreign affairs administrator of the German Evangelical Church he was shortly to become Bonhoeffer's superior [when

he went to London]. Novi Sad and Sofia revealed the extent to which the two men's paths were diverging. For Heckel now pursued a quite different course in his attempt to steer safely into the harbour that rudderless ship, the German Church and her congregations abroad. Though he was never to join the German Christians, yet he continued to hazard his reputation throughout the Nazi period, and, indeed, was to lose it irretrievably so far as Bonhoeffer and his friends at home and abroad were concerned. In Bonhoeffer's eyes Heckel's way was tantamount to surrender, for his policy seemed like a betrayal of the Church and the ecumenical movement."[2]

The Executive Committee of Life and Work met in Novi Sad and Heckel was the spokesman for the German party. He had a very difficult task. He was looking both ways – towards the Synod of his own church and towards the representatives of foreign churches. By September 1933, enough had happened to Germany to cause disquiet in other lands, particularly the Aryan Clause which excluded from the Ministry those of Jewish origin. An extract from the minutes of the Executive Committee of Life and Work was reproduced in Siegmund-Schultze's journal "Die Eiche":

> "Heckel painted a clear picture of the vast changes and preliminary reconstruction in Nation, State and Church, and sought to clarify the great questions and tasks which hereby assume particular importance for the whole work of the churches in the ecumenical field."[3]

Wilfred Monod, representing France, objected to Heckel's report and expressed concern that he had said nothing about the disabilities imposed upon Jewish Christians. There was a heated debate and two resolutions were passed with which the Germans disagreed. George Bell was in the chair and he was disturbed to find such a division, but he insisted upon the wording of a resolution which he brought forward with all his knowledge of events in Germany and their background:

> "Grave anxieties were expressed by the representatives of different churches in Europe and America, in particular with regard to the severe action taken against persons of Jewish origin, and the serious restrictions placed upon freedom of thought and expression in Germany . . ."[4]

The second resolution committed Bell to write a letter to the German Church governing body. This he did on the 23rd October and started a correspondence with Ludwig Müller (Hitler's nominee .for National Bishop). That correspondence went on until Bell's Ascension Day message in 1934. It is of considerable importance for understanding both George Bell and the German Church struggle.

An Intimate Friendship

Not long after the conferences in Sofia and Novi Sad, Bonhoeffer decided to leave Germany and take pastoral responsibility for two German-speaking congregations in London. He began his duties with the congregation in Sydenham on 17th October 1933 and almost at once he was in touch with the Bishop of Chichester. The growing relationship between the two men is reflected in the continuous correspondence (in English) between them. It began with an invitation to come to Church House, Brighton on 21st November which Bonhoeffer readily accepted. in the letter of acceptance, he at once explains that he knows how well informed Bell is about the German situation and warns him that a split is likely in the National Church, which could become a strongly political issue and would be treated as such. Hence he points out that it is very important that the ecumenical movement should refuse to recognise the National Church.

> "If the ecumenical movement would keep silent during these days, I am afraid that all trust put into it by the minority would be destroyed."

And he adds:

> "Müller is now in a very precarious position and a strong demand from the side of the ecumenical churches could be the last hope for the Christian churches in Germany."[5]

Bell was prepared for this by the report of a private meeting that Bonhoeffer had had in Sofia with a group from the conference in an hotel room. They had discussed the 'real' situation in Germany and the group instructed Bonhoeffer to tell his friends:

> "1. that they can count on our sympathy and understanding abroad,
> 2. that in principle it would be necessary for a delegation to decide whether the churches are able to recognise the new German Church."[6]

Bonhoeffer made his own report within two weeks of settling in London to Siegmund-Schultze.

26

"Incidentally during this little meeting we decided on a plan to send a delegation to the German Church government, and this is still under discussion here in London."[7]

That then was Bonhoeffer's hope – that the ecumenical movement would not recognise the German National Church, but declare with him that the Confessing Church, the minority split which resisted the inroads of 'German Christian' and Nazi philosophy into the Church, was the authentic Protestant Church in Germany.

In his letter to Bell, Bonhoeffer pressed home his appeal for the Confessing Church:

"We must not leave alone these men who fight – humanly speaking – an almost hopeless struggle."

He adds:

"I get news with every mail and also by telephone. If I may I will forward to you the recent information."

And he enclosed some good examples of what he calls "the formulations of the Teutonic Christians".[8]

George Bell was responsive and told him that he had not only written to Müller, but published the letter in full in the *Manchester Guardian*, and substantial parts in *The Times*. This was to be Bell's strategy. He did not argue only with the churches, but informed the public. He made good use of the press and later of the House of Lords. To Bonhoeffer, he sent a copy of the English original and the German translation. They therefore had much to discuss. Bonhoeffer arrived in Brighton on 21st November and after tea returned with Bell to Chichester, where he stayed two days.

Bonhoeffer was completely satisfied that he had found an influential companion and father in George Bell. His letters were sent almost daily to keep the Bishop informed. From these letters we can gather how Bonhoeffer and therefore Bell went up and down in their hopes for the Confessing Church and the fall of Müller. Bell could not have had a better informant and he soon saw the quality of Bonhoeffer's mind as well as his complete integrity. He trusted him totally.

When the editor of *The Round Table* asked Bell for an article for the March issue of his journal in 1934, the Bishop recommended Bonhoeffer as best able to write the article which was to be on 'The Crisis in the German Protestant Church'. After giving details of his qualifications for the task, he added:

"He knows the personnel of the German Church in Berlin extremely well and is a follower of Karl Barth. He is also in almost daily touch with the situation in Berlin. Further, he is one of the earliest members of the Pastors' Emergency League, now swollen to 6,000 members, and his name is actually the first of the twenty or so signatures to the famous manifesto which the Pastors' Emergency League presented to the Prussian Synod in September. I do not think you could get anyone to write an article of the kind you want with more authority, and you can be very certain of his ability. I would gladly help him in any way that was useful. He and I would probably discuss the article together, as he is coming to stay with me again shortly."[9]

Bonhoeffer declined to write the article. He was already suspected of giving information to *The Times*, either directly or through Bell, and this further involvement would have been dangerous.

A Dangerous Friendship

The developing friendship between George Bell and the young German pastor caused some alarm in Berlin. About the personal nature of the friendship there was no doubt. It was almost a father-son relationship. In fact, when Hildebrandt joined Bonhoeffer, Bell referred to them as 'my two boys'. Many years later this affection is still evident. It is expressed in the Introduction which Bell wrote to the *Cost of Discipleship* (English Translation of Bonhoeffer's *Nachfolge*):

"I knew him in London in the early days of the evil regime and from him, more than any other German, I learned the true character of the conflict, in an intimate friendship."[10]

The source of that intimate friendship was succinctly expressed in the same introduction:

"He was crystal clear in his convictions; and young as he was, and humble-minded as he was, he saw the truth and spoke it with a complete absence of fear."

The friendship was mutual. Dietrich Bonhoeffer turned to Bell more than once in the crises of his life and regarded him as a father confessor at times, but always as a father.

Bonhoeffer recognised Bell's strength, but sometimes overestimated his influence. He wanted Bell to persuade the ecumenical movement to decide between the two church bodies.[11] It had no power to do so and Bell could not go as far as Bonhoeffer wanted him to. He persuaded the ecumenical movement to condemn what was happening in Germany and to criticise the actions of the 'German Christians'. But constitutionally it could not decide that the National Church of Germany was inadmissible.

Bell did all he could – and perhaps more than he should. The fellowship in no way suffered. Both men loved and respected each other. But there was danger in this influential closeness. Eberhard Bethge lists four matters on which Bonhoeffer was suspect as being too influential and supplying the press and the church leaders with too much information.[12]

1. It was rumoured that Bonhoeffer was connected with the accurate reporting in *The Times*.
2. Bell, who eventually wrote the article for *The Round Table*, was helped considerably by Bonhoeffer in the writing of so accurate a description of the crisis in the German Protestant Church.
3. The correspondence between Bell and Bishop Ludwig Müller which grew more critical was said to be encouraged by the information supplied by Bonhoeffer.
4. Of all the German dignitaries, only Bonhoeffer was received by the Archbishop of Canterbury.

When it was learned that Bell as the chairman of Life and Work intended to call a conference for private discussion on the position of the Church in Germany and that Bonhoeffer was involved, Theodore Heckel, now a bishop and head of the 'Church Office for External Affairs', summoned him back to Berlin and tried to submit him to an authority which he would not accept. Heckel would have liked to bring him back permanently from London, but failed. To his friend Sutz in Switzerland, Bonhoeffer wrote, "They'd give anything to get me away from here, and, if only for that reason, I am digging my heels in".[13]

The Correspondence with Ludwig Müller

The first letter from George Bell to Ludwig Müller was sent in January 1934.[14] It was unexpectedly well informed about the situation in Germany (thanks largely to Bonhoeffer) and it was frank and official.

In the name of the Universal Christian Council for Life and Work he reminded the Reich Bishop that he had promised a repeal of the Aryan paragraph and the violent measures against Christians of Jewish origin. Instead, the so-called "muzzling decree" had done just the opposite. It was not a personal letter, but with the express permission of the Executive Committee of Life and Work, and it appeared in *The Times* on 1st February 1934. Berlin was embarrassed and Müller saw that his policy of maintaining good relations with other churches, while restricting the information they received, was in tatters. About the same time, the Swedish Archbishop Erling Eidem was equally well informed, thanks to Birger Forell, pastor at the Swedish Embassy in Berlin.

Theodor Heckel came as quickly as he could to London. There, in February he tried to obtain – from the pastors of the German congregations in Britain – 'a common declaration of loyalty to the Reich Bishop'. Thanks largely to Bonhoeffer he failed. He visited the Bishop of Chichester and asked him for a six-month truce until things calmed down in Germany. Bell was much disturbed by the proposed "Reich Ministry for relations with the Evangelical Church", to which Heckel was to be appointed head, because he saw it as a further restriction on the liberty of the German-speaking churches in Britain. Bell spoke as chairman of Life and Work and refused to keep silence, as Heckel had wished, until 'pacification' had been achieved. Heckel returned with no more than the promise of a joint investigation into the problems with which the churches were concerned. Bell gave him also some 'informal notes' listing the charges against the National Church in Germany. In his later letters, Bell expounded these charges with detailed examples (some provided by Bonhoeffer). He wrote two letters and received no answer. Bell decided to make a public statement and on 29th March published this in *The Times*. This was the frankest of all his statements, expressing his continuing serious doubts about the National Church, which he claimed had been increased by news of recent events. This gave great encouragement to the Confessing Church and efforts were made to involve Bell in the Church Struggle in Germany.

Chairman of the World Alliance

When George Bell went to Oud Wassenaar in October 1919 it was as a member of the Anglican Delegation to the first post-war meeting of the International Committee of the World Alliance for Promoting International Friendship through the Churches. The leader of the delegation was Bishop Talbot of Winchester. The financial resources of the whole ecumenical movement were dependent upon the World Alliance which appealed for funds among the Peace movements. Bell's courageous resolution on peace and the outright condemnation of war, urging churches to refuse to support a government which did not accept negotiations first, took him into the heart of the Peace movements and the World Alliance. He was undoubtedly a leading and trusted figure among them after the Eisenach Conference in September 1929, from which his resolution came. He saw the need however, for the three streams of the ecumenical movement to come together for effective action. The Continuation Committee of Life and Work, set up in Stockholm in 1927 began to feel the need for a permanent body – the Universal Christian Council for Life and Work. A small group, under Bell's leadership was set up to work out a constitution. Bell's first proposal was for an Executive Committee to handle the continuing work, and the Council to concentrate on major issues when it met. The third element was Faith and Order. At Chezbres in September 1930, the Executive Committee reorganised itself and a small group representative of Faith and Order, Life and Work and the World Alliance was formed under Bell's chairmanship to work out closer cooperation. All three had secretaries in Geneva. Bell strove to unite them all. He felt that the churches would not support three ecumenical organisations. At this point, Bell argued first for the uniting of Faith and Order with the World Alliance. Geneva was hesitant. Then Bell found himself in the chair of Life and Work. Bishop Theodore Woods of Winchester died after only one year as president of the British Section on 27th February 1932. Bell succeeded him and was at once made chairman of the Council. This made him chairman at the time of the annual meeting at Geneva in August 1932, where his term of office was extended for a further two years to enable him to prepare the Second World Conference on Faith and Order in 1937. Long before that he was chairman of the World Alliance and of the Executive Committee of Life and Work. When he spoke now, it was for the Ecumenical Movement and no longer simply for the Anglican delegation.

Plans for a Free Synod

The Confessing Church had not yet held a National Synod. Sooner or later they would have to organise an alternative to the National Church if they were to be recognised in place of it. There were other much stronger reasons why the Confessing Church should establish its opposition to the National Church and define its theological objectives. It was not on political, but on theological grounds that it must stand and fight. Bell understood this. When Bonhoeffer was summoned to Berlin in March 1934 he learned of the increasing tensions and anxieties and of plans for a Free National Synod. Back in London, he informed Bell of the plans and handed him a request that the mother churches of the Universal Council for Life and Work should not support the National Church. On 30th April, the Bishop visited the German Ambassador, Leopold von Hoesch, to complain to him, in the name of the churches outside Germany, of the autocratic rule of the Reich Bishop. It was a strong protest in which Bell pointed out that further such developments would lead to the Council having to break off relations with Germany. Hoesch was himself a devout Protestant from an old Reformed family and he left no doubt in his report that a warning sign was being given to the Foreign Office in Berlin.

On 10th May, Ascension Day, the Bishop published his message to the ecumenical churches. It was an official message headed:

> "A Message Regarding the German Evangelical Church to the Representatives of the Churches of the Universal Christian Council for Life and Work from the Bishop of Chichester."[15]

The message condemned the *Führer* principle and the autocratic rule of the National Bishop, as "without precedent in the history of the Church".

The message was not given official publicity in Germany, but it was not censored. It was quoted freely in the church papers close to the opposition. The letter was a catalogue of grievances against the National Church and was in unequivocal terms. Although Bell did not and could not interfere with the internal affairs of a national church, nor could he issue an ultimatum, he made no secret of his dislike of practices which he described as "incompatible with Christian principles". The message did not say all that Bonhoeffer wanted, but he was unstinted in his praise for the fact that "in its conciseness it strikes at the main points and leaves no escape for misinterpretation".[16]

It was clear from this pastoral letter, addressed to all the churches of the ecumenical movement, that Bell was attempting to place that movement behind the opposition to the National Church in Germany. Its significance was not missed, either in Germany, where the National Church did not react except by abuse, or by the opposition which took heart, as well as throughout the ecumenical movement preparing for an international conference that summer. The events that followed the sending of the letter make that abundantly clear. For Bell's role in the Church Struggle in Germany it is necessary to study the full text.

The Message

> "I have been urged from many quarters to issue some statement to my fellow members of the Universal Christian Council for Life and Work upon the present position in the German Evangelical Church, especially as it affects other Churches represented on the Universal Council for Life and Work.
>
> "The situation is, beyond doubt, full of anxiety. To estimate it aright we have to remember the fact that a revolution has taken place in the German state, and that as a necessary result the German Evangelical Church was bound to be faced with new tasks and many new problems requiring time for their full solution. It is nonetheless true that the present position is being watched by members of the Christian Church abroad not only with great interest, but with a deepening concern. The chief cause of anxiety is the assumption by the Reich Bishop, in the

name of the leadership principle, of autocratic powers unqualified by constitutional or traditional restraints which are without precedent in the history of the Church. The exercise of these autocratic powers by the Church government appears incompatible with the Christian principle of seeking in brotherly fellowship to receive the guidance of the Holy Spirit. It has had disastrous results on the internal unity of the Church and the disciplinary measures which have been taken by Church government against Ministers of the Gospel on account of their loyalty to the fundamental principles of Christian truth, have made a painful impression on Christian opinion abroad, already disturbed by the introduction of racial discrimination in the universal fellowship of the Christian Church. No wonder that voices should be raised in Germany itself making a solemn pronouncement before the whole Christian world on the dangers which the spiritual life of the Evangelical Church is facing, which are the common concern of the whole of Christendom.

"These are such fundamental questions as those respecting the nature of the Church, its witness, its freedom and its relation to the secular power. At the end of August the Universal Council will be meeting in Denmark. The agenda will inevitably include a consideration of the religious issues raised by the present situation in the German Evangelical Church. It will also have to consider the wider questions which affect the life of all the Churches in Christendom. A committee met last month in Paris to prepare for its work, and its report will shortly be published entitled "The Church, the State and World Order". I hope that this meeting will assist the Churches in their friendship with each other, and in their task of reaching a common mind on the implications of their faith in relation to the dominant tendencies in modern thought and society, and in particular to the growing demands of the modern State. The times are critical. Something beyond conferences and consultations is required. We need as never before to turn our thoughts and spirits to God. More earnest efforts must be made in our theological study. Above all more humble and fervent prayer must be offered to our Father in Heaven. May He, who knows our weakness and our blindness, through a new outpouring of the Spirit, enable the whole Church to bear its witness to its Lord with courage and faith!"

(signed) George Cicestr
Ascensiontide 1934

The Message brings out the wide range of issues with which Bell was addressing the members of the Universal Council and the intention he had to raise these issues at the forthcoming conference in Denmark. There is first the anxiety and deep concern about the autocratic powers of the National Bishop, and the way these powers were being exercised.

He then points out the dangers of division and puts himself on the side of the opposition. One of the things that the conference in Denmark will have to face is its attitude to the National Church and to the opposition. The warning that the issue of the German Evangelical Church will be placed on the agenda is clear. Racial discrimination is deliberately listed at a time when even the BBC was muzzled lest the 'Dictators' be offended. The whole message tells of an active and informed ecumenical movement which intends to act. The Paris Committee also indicated that the machinery is in motion and a report is promised.

The Effect of the Message

Bell's direct reference to the unacceptable powers of the National Bishop and his objection to the way in which that autocratic power was being used must have weakened Müller's position. Bell had exposed the purpose of the office of the National Bishop with unprecedented powers as a means of state control of the Church. At this time, Hitler was attempting to build a continental empire and he wanted no early quarrel with the British Maritime Empire or with the United States. This message was one more piece of evidence that Müller was an embarrassment.

Even more important than the criticism of the National Church was the support given to those voices "making a solemn pronouncement before the whole Christian world on the dangers to which the spiritual life of the Evangelical Church is exposed". They were voices "raised in Germany itself", not interference from outside. The Confessing Church took heart from it as they prepared for the First Free Synod of the Confessing Church in Barmen two weeks later.

Theodor Heckel's experience at Novi Sad worried him and it was not good news that the same issues would be raised at the forthcoming conference in Denmark. It was by now crystal clear to him that Bonhoeffer had a powerful champion in the chairman of the Universal Council.

Ludwig Müller was also aware that this was not merely a further letter in a unilateral correspondence, but addressed to all the member churches of the Universal Council. He could ignore it, but he was aware that it was influencing other churches abroad – particularly in Denmark where the crisis in German Protestantism was clearly understood already by Ammundsen, who would be host to the forthcoming conference on the Danish island of Fanö. Müller was also aware that others beside him and even politically superior to him had read the Message with concern. There was no official answer from Germany, but Bell's authority was recognised. Official documents make reference to him and in November he was visited in Chichester by Hitler's envoy extraordinary Herr von Ribbentrop.

Barmen

The Synod at Barmen met 29th–31st May 1934. The Pastors' Emergency League was now the Confessing Church. In German the name is Bekennende Kirche (BK) and it was a national organisation.

Bonhoeffer insisted and Bell agreed that it was not a 'movement' but a Church. At Barmen it held its first National Synod with a sense of ecumenical solidarity. With this support the Synod confidently wrote the Confession, necessary "in view of the destructive errors of the German Christians". The Barmen Confession pledged members of the Confessing Church to the basic evangelical truths and spelt out where the 'German Christians' had departed from them. It is a long document and worthy of careful study. Its best known assertion which had clear relevance in Nazi Germany was:

> "We repudiate the false teaching that there are areas of life in which we belong not to Jesus Christ, but to some other lord, areas in which we do not need justification and sanctification through him."[17]

Neither Bonhoeffer nor Bell were present at Barmen, but both were informed by representatives whom they trusted. Bonhoeffer had his friend Karl Barth who was almost the architect of the conference and author of the Confession. It was a Barthian document! Bonhoeffer early expressed his dissatisfaction with the total absence of any reference to the treatment of the Jews. When he raised this protest, he was told that it was not opportune to refer to such controversial matters which might weaken their case! Bell's contribution was very much the Ascensiontide Message, but he too was disappointed that the Confession paid no attention to the violation of 'oneness in Christ', which ruled out any racial discrimination in the Church. He had clearly made this point in his Message, but it was absent in the Barmen Confession. Historians who praise the courage of Barmen, have to this day to confess that it was silent about the Jews.

The Misunderstanding of Bonhoeffer

The Ascensiontide Message had made direct reference to the forthcoming meeting of the Universal Council in Denmark, where the crisis in the German Protestant Church would have to have a place on the agenda. Together with the report of the Paris meeting, "The Church, the State and World Order", it was Bell's Message which determined the Agenda in Denmark.

It became clear that Bell was one of the few people who understood the deep concern of Bonhoeffer that the Confessing Church should accept its role as the Church and not simply 'the opposition'. Bethge confesses that Bonhoeffer was difficult to understand on this point when he repeatedly emphasised the significance of the Sermon on the Mount in the Church Struggle. Equally he confused others by his inisistence upon the Confession and the need to refute heresy. This double emphasis isolated him from his brethren in Barmen. Bell showed his nearness to Bonhoeffer most clearly in his sympathy with him on these two points. He himself had had to contend for a theological undergirding of the Life and Work movement and had hammered out his own theological position with Germans at the Anglo-German Theological Conferences. While many in the ecumenical movement could be stirred to indignation by practical affairs and examples of injustice in Germany, Bell saw the value of Bonhoeffer's refusal to use such 'sensational' material to deal with basically theological questions. Bethge maintains that the way in which many at Barmen were using the name 'Confessing Church', but meaning 'the opposition', was incomprehensible to Bonhoeffer and adds that his "analysis and conception met with sympathy and understanding in Bell".[18] That comment is of very great importance for understanding Bell's unique grasp of the situation in the German Evangelical Church, and the spiritual dangers to which it was exposed.

He recognised the importance of the Confession and for that reason had it printed in full in *The Times* on 4th June 1934. Years later, when he wrote the Preface to the English translation of Bonhoeffer's *The Cost of Discipleship*, the book dealing primarily with the Sermon on the Mount, he shows his understanding of Bonhoeffer's insistence that we cannot depart from it. Even in 1934, Bell understood Bonhoeffer's need to battle against cheap grace. So as both men prepared for the meeting of the Universal Council in Denmark in August 1934 they were theologically at one.

Bell's deep concern for peace had also influenced Bonhoeffer who had met the ecumenical movement in America largely in the form of the Peace Movement and had been influenced towards a pacifist position there by his fellow-student from France, Jean Lazerre.

Nineteen Thirty-Four in Germany

The events described so far took place against a background of revolution in Germany and although it was in 1933 that Hitler came to power, the year of clarification and of the first horrific moves of the Dictator was 1934.

Klaus Scholder, in his *The Churches and the Third Reich,* devoted the whole of his second volume to 1934 and even then did not complete the year. He called it "The Year of Disillusionment", in which "all the hopes of 1934 were shattered one by one".[19]

A cynical non-aggression pact with Poland was signed while Hitler paid attention to other borders; central government deprived provincial governments of important powers; Himmler took over the Secret Police (Gestapo); Hitler and Mussolini met in Venice to strengthen an 'axis' for the future of Europe; the liquidation of the crack SA troops (SA = Sturmabteilung, which Ernst Röhm had raised in August 1921 to launch Hitler, but which seemed to him in 1934 to threaten him); the murder of Ernst Röhm and 207 of his leading men in "the night of the long knives"; Hindenburg died and Hitler combined the two highest offices in his own person to become an all-powerful Dictator, both Führer and Reich Chancellor of Germany; laws were passed to give him more and more power; Dolfuss was assassinated in Austria, which began to look like an extension of Hitler's Germany.

The resilience of the German Protestant Opposition was all the more remarkable in such a year. At the first anniversary of Hitler's rise to power in January, the Opposition seemed beaten and the western press with few exceptions saw Hitler as the 'right man for Germany'. Yet, Barmen took place in May of that year and now in August the decisive battle for ecumenical support was staged on the Danish island of Fanö.

The World Conference at Fanö

Under Bell's leadership the ecumenical movement was increasingly restless at what was going on in Germany. The Ascension Day Message had given a signal, but more decisive action was needed. The turning point was the ecumenical conference planned for the end of August 1934. It was organised jointly by the Universal Council for Life and Work and the World Alliance for Promoting International Friendship through the Churches. There was an ecumenical Youth Conference planned to run parallel with it. As President of the Council, Bell had a difficult problem over the delegations to the Conference. Member churches all elected their own representatives. But Bell knew and had made clear in his Message that the German Protestant Church was divided. It was extremely unlikely that Theodor Heckel would nominate anyone from the Confessing Church, especially as the ecumenical attitude to the German Evangelical Church was on the Agenda. This was recognised as a problem as early as June when Bell encouraged Bonhoeffer (still a pastor in London) to travel to Berlin to discuss a Confessing Church delegation with Karl Koch (the Praeses of Westfalen) and Martin Niemöller.

Although personally Bonhoeffer was against the representation of the National Church, the others persuaded him that it was necessary to accept the facts of life and agree to two delegations. He returned with a list of delegates from the Confessing Church. Bonhoeffer maintained his personal point by writing to Geneva and saying that there could be only one youth delegation and the ecumenical movement must decide which Church it will recognise! That was unrealistic. The ecumenical movement could not fail to invite the National Church however much they disapproved of it. Bell invited two delegations and explained the problem to Koch. The invitation was carefully worded. Koch was invited to bring a delegation "as guests and as authoritative spokesmen in a very difficult situation". He pointed out that a discussion on the German Protestant Church situation could only be conducted with both sides present. But this caused confusion and the Confessing Church refused to take part in the Fanö Conference. Like Barth, they thought the time was approaching when Germans would have to choose between Christianity and National Socialism. Others felt the impossibility of speaking frankly in the presence of delegates of the National Church. With Theodor Heckel present there could be no "off the record". Bell took what steps he could. He sent Ammundsen to Hamburg to discuss the problem with Koch, Fielder and Hildebrandt but he could not change their minds.

Meanwhile Heckel had heard of the invitation, but not of the refusal by the Confessing Church. He asked Bell "on the basis of what regulations of the constitution and standing orders" the invitation had been issued. Bell justified his action as one taken in consultation with the relevant officials under the constitution which allowed the President to exercise such powers 'in cases of emergency'. Heckel complained that the Council was not competent to discuss German internal affairs. Eventually Bell invited Koch and Bonhoeffer to the Council as individuals. Koch declined for various good reasons. Bonhoeffer accepted with alacrity.

Bell's own account of that Conference is perhaps all that we need. He describes it briefly in "The Kingship of Christ", when he is writing about 'National Socialism and the Church':

> "When the Universal Council itself met at Fanö in Denmark in 1934, the situation had become worse. There was an extra-ordinary scene when a Nazi courier came by air from quarters attached to the new government in Germany, with instructions to the German Church delegates. The whole atmosphere of this meeting was tense, as there were anti-Nazi Germans secretly present as well as official delegates of the Evangelical Church. Discussion in closed session was extremely animated, reports

were somehow reaching the outside world through American press agencies and causing a great stir.

The Council expressed its criticism of the Nazi regime in clear terms. Strong support was given to the resistance movement in the *Confessional* [Bell always used this for the *Confessing*] Church; and while the council also expressed the desire to remain in friendly contact with all groups in the German Evangelical Church, it added Praeses Koch and Dietrich Bonhoeffer to its membership as a special sign of its resolve to maintain close fellowship with the Confessional Church."[20]

It was at this conference that Bonhoeffer gave his now famous 'peace sermon' which inspired action half a century later in the 'eighties. The influence of George Bell is evident throughout, although the style is more that of Deissmann, and the sermon bears distinct resemblance to the resolution Bell persuaded the "Christ and Peace" meeting to pass in 1929. He too had called for political action by the churches, even to the extent of non-cooperation if the government refused to negotiate before going to war.

Bonhoeffer was more dramatic but along the same lines:

"How does the peace come about? Through a system of political treaties? Through the investment of international capital in different countries? Through the big banks, through money? Or through universal peaceful rearmament in order to guarantee peace? Through none of these, for the single reason that in all of them peace is confused with safety. There is no way to peace along the way of safety. For peace must be dared, it is the great venture. Which of us can say he knows what it might mean for the world if one nation should meet the aggressor, not with weapons in hand, but praying, defenceless and for that very reason protected by a bulwark never failing? . . . Why do we fear the fury of the world powers? Why don't we take the power from them and give it back to Christ? We can still do it today. The Ecumenical Council is in session, it can send out to all believers this radical call to peace. The nations are waiting for it in the East and in the West. Must we be put to shame by non-Christian people in the East? Shall we desert the individuals who are risking their lives for this message? The hour is late. The world is choked with weapons, and dreadful is the distrust which looks out of all men's eyes. The trumpets of war may blow tomorrow. For what are we waiting? Do we want to become involved in this guilt as never before?"[21]

George Bell heard something of his own self in that appeal. The conference, of course, passed on, but he never forgot the sincerity and good sense of that call.

Theodor Heckel felt lost until the arrival of the airborne messenger, who at first he thought was to inform him of his dismissal. He argued manfully for the recognition of the National Church and succeeded, although close fellowship was still to be maintained with the Confessing Church. What Bell saw as more important than these relationships and recognition was the decision to tackle the major issues. On the initiative of Dr. J. H. Oldham, the Council decided to direct the attention of the Churches to the emergence of crucial and urgent issues concerning Church, Community and State, as well as the conflict between Christianity and Secularism. What had been happening to Germany showed how acute could be the conflict between Church and State still in the twentieth century. It was this that, to use Bell's own words, "gave the main direction to the future character of the ecumenical movement on the Life and Work side".

The Stockholm Conference in 1925 had dealt with a large number of contemporary questions, international, racial, social, educational; but its focus was not clear. The wonder was that it happened at all and Bell maintains that it would not have done, but for the enthusiasm of Archbishop Söderblom. He puts this down to "his vision . . . his vitality, his powers of persuasion, his leadership and inspiration".[22] The next Life and Work conference, which was planned for 1937 was to be quite different. It had a theme which all its member churches knew was relevant and urgent. This change was effected largely by confronting the situation in Germany and discussing the crisis in the Protestant Church there.

The Second Conference on Life and Work

The location was Oxford in 1937: "Church, Community and State" was the theme. The problems were graver than those which Stockholm had faced and the whole international situation was far more serious. The delegation from the Confessing Church in Germany had been prevented from attending. Bell saw to it that a special message of fellowship was sent to them and it was largely his drafting. It expressed the concern of the whole conference and very much that of George Bell personally when it said that they were

> "greatly moved by the afflictions of many pastors and laymen who had stood firm from the first in the Confessional Church for the sovereignty of Christ, and for the freedom of the Church of Christ to preach the Gospel."

1937 was only three years after the conference at Fanö and the situation in Germany had become worse.

1934–1937: from Fanö to Oxford

After some hope that the 'German Christians' were tottering and that Hitler's plan for the National Church was abandoned, there followed a very serious period for the Protestant Churches of Southern Germany which even brought the sympathy of the Catholics in an area where relations between the two Confessions had been very bad indeed. The attack on Meiser, the Protestant Bishop of Bavaria, and attempts to remove him led to demonstrations in Franconia (the strongly Protestant part of Bavaria) unique in the Third Reich. It soon became clear that a nationwide attack on the Confessing Church was about to be launched; but Bavaria had shown that it could be resisted by the people and soon grow wider than the church sphere. There was real fear of strong opposition and Hitler needed a time of domestic peace to prepare for the plebiscite which would bring the Saarland back to Germany. At this time he also wanted the support of Britain.

Bell decided that it was time for intervention. He had been commissioned to maintain close contacts with the Confessing Church by resolutions at Fanö. He took these seriously and at the end of September met Praeses Koch and other members of the Confessing Church for an extended conversation. He learned of the trouble in South Germany and that a new National Synod of the Confessing Church was planned for October. Koch asked for a representative from the Universal Council to be present and thus express solidarity with the Confessing Church in the spirit of Fanö. Bell asked his friend, Alphons Koechlin, President of the Swiss Protestant Church Alliance, to undertake this task. Meanwhile news came through of the deposition of the Landesbischof of Württemberg and the attack on the Bavarian Church. Bell decided that the situation was serious enough for him to undertake a diplomatic intervention on behalf of the beleaguered Confessing Church and others in opposition. He consulted with Cosmo Lang, Archbishop of Canterbury, and on 12th October went to see the German *chargé d'affaires* in London, Count von Bismarck, to inform him that if the news from Southern Germany were accurate 'an imminent public declaration of a complete break between all the Protestant Churches abroad and the German churches led by the Reich Bishop was unavoidable'. Bismarck, who at once sent off a report of the conversation to Berlin, added that,

> "the Bishop's visit showed once again the decisive significance
> constantly expressed in the embassy reports, of a speedy

settlement of the church conflict. This is absolutely necessary if relations between England and Germany are to be improved."[23]

This caused some alarm in the Foreign Office in Berlin and the Foreign Minister warned that it might hinder Germany's rearmament plans. Hitler hesitated. The Archbishop of Canterbury decided to support Bell by a spectacular step of his own. On 16th October he invited the German Ambassador to an interview and repeated to him much of what Bell had said to the *chargé d'affaires*. But in addition he added that there was a meeting of English Bishops on 24th October at which he was required to make a statement about relations with the German National Church. He indicated that there would be consultation with the Scandinavian Bishops and that he would propose joint action with the Catholics to Cardinal Bourne unless Germany changed its church policy. Of course, he assured the German Ambassador that he was in no way thinking of bringing pressure to bear or threats! He made it clear that a complete break with Germany was inevitable unless some steps were taken, such as "the repeal of measures against Bishops Meiser, Wurm and Dr. Koch and the removal of Dr. Jäger (State Commissar of Prussia, appointed to put an end to strife within the Church)".

This double intervention of Bell and Lang was effective. Bonhoeffer was back in London and close to Bell. A letter written by him to Bell on 24th October in the midst of this is of very great interest:

"With regard to the recent and expected events in the German church, I am afraid that Hitler will try to postpone a decision as long as possible – perhaps even until after the Saar election. I could imagine him saying that he would not interfere in the Church conflict, not even in the situation of a schism. He would leave it all to the Church and, of course, in fact, leave it to some 'Nazi' groups to interfere on their own initiative and so to terrorise the Evangelical Church in Germany. I have been thinking much more about your question, what Hitler could do in case he was willing to settle the conflict. From his point of view I can only see the one way of dismissing Jäger and Müller and nominating a representative of the Opposition – possibly a lawyer, not a theologian, Dr. Klor of the *Reichgerichte* (the supreme court) – with the special task to restitute legal and confessional conditions in the church. After a certain period of vacancy, a new *Reichbischof* might be appointed elected by a legal National Synod. This interim however should last for at least one year, so that the greatest excitement might have passed. There is a certain difficulty of Hitler nominating a theologian who would become *Reichbischof* afterwards. We have always disapproved of the nomination of Müller, not only personally, but also fundamentally. He may nominate a lawyer, but he has just to confirm a theologian."[24]

That was the kind of advice and information that Bell received from Bonhoeffer and he used it wisely. But time was passing and Bonhoeffer could not continue indefinitely in London.

The Departure of Bonhoeffer

When at Fanö Bonhoeffer talked about the courage of non-resistance to aggression and added, "Must we be put to shame by non-Christian people in the East?" he clearly had Gandhi in mind. Bell provided him with an introduction to Gandhi and wrote preparing the way for a visit:

"A friend of mine, a young man, at present German pastor in London, Pastor Bonhoeffer, 23 Manor Mount, London SE23, is most anxious that I should give him an introduction to you. I can most heartedly commend him. He expects to be in India for the first two or three months of 1935. He is intimately identified with the church opposition movement in Germany. He is a very good theologian, a most earnest man, and is probably to have charge of the training of ordination candidates for the ministry in the future Confessing Church of Germany. He wants to study community life as well as methods of training. It would be a very great kindness if you could let him come to you."[25]

That was written on the 22nd October when Bell and Bonhoeffer were both deeply involved in the issues of the church policy in Germany. It is indicative of Bell's wide range of interests and his readiness to help a friend on a purely personal matter. The letter also gives us the first reference to the possibility of Bonhoeffer's recall to Germany for a specific task. However, he was never to make the journey to India. On 16th April, he and his first students made their way along the dunes of the Baltic, by Zingst, to their primitive cabins. Bonhoeffer, disappointed of India and the lessons he might learn from Gandhi, proceeded to form his own ashram and prepared for Finkewalde.[26]

Bell missed him, although they kept in contact, but never again were they to experience the ease of relationship they had known during Bonhoeffer's two years in London.

Bell's Involvement in Germany

Although Bonhoeffer had returned to Germany to undertake seminary work for the Confessing Church, he was still regarded as its best contact with the Bishop of Chichester. Praeses Koch asked Bonhoeffer to go to England twice during his first summer in Finkewalde. The purpose of the first was to inform Bell that a secret meeting of the Confessing Church was scheduled for 22nd May in Gohlfeld. Would Bell send a greeting? At the same time the precarious situation made necessary some cryptic messages. One was that if the meeting was broken up Bell should proceed at once to Berlin and meet for discussion with Koechlin and friends of the Confessing Church. That was on the 18th May. Bonhoeffer's second visit was also to brief the Bishop of Chichester, who was now regarded as the spokesman for the Confessing Church outside Germany. This second visit took place in the first two weeks of August 1935. There were two reasons for it. The one concerned the meeting planned for August 1936, the last meeting of Life and Work before the World Conference in Oxford in the following year. The Provisional Church Administration of the Confessing Church had decided not to attend the meeting, because Heckel would be there. The second reason was that Bell had decided to follow up the visit Ribbentrop had made to him, in June 1935, when he had promised that he would introduce him to Hitler's Deputy, Rudolf Hess and to Hanns Kerrl, the newly appointed Minister for Church Affairs. For this Bell had to be briefed and there was no one he trusted more than Bonhoeffer. There were also currency matters to be discussed in view of Germany's strict controls. Bell intended to meet Hess and Kerrl fully informed. He had to see Bonhoeffer to arrange this. The post was no longer reliable or safe. Both these meetings were helpful to Bell and a joy to them both. Bonhoeffer was the warrior who would accept no compromise, but he was tempered by Bell whose quiet persistence and consistent belief in people kept hope alive. Bell did see Rudolf Hess at his home in Berlin and pointed out to him that the World Church needed the German Evangelical Church for its fight against the non-Christian elements in the world. Hess read this as the fight against Bolshevism. Bell probably had secularism in mind as his later writing in *Christianity and World Order*[27] shows at the very beginning. But it provided common ground for a moment between the Deputy Führer and the Bishop of Chichester and may have been one of the elements contributing to that strange flight of Rudolf Hess during the subsequent war. Bell tells us that Frau Hess, who had been very critical of him until that point, exclaimed, "Oh, that is why foreign Churches are interested in our Church conflict". From that point on, she and her husband warmed to Bell's questions and, as he says, they both fully agreed that it was the business of the Church to unite their forces against anti-God and anti-Christianity. The conversations were interrupted by the arrival of Hitler, but Rudolf Hess expressed the wish for further contacts.[28]

44

Notes

1. G. K. A. Bell, *A Brief Sketch of the Church of England*, SCM Press, London, 1929.
2. Eberhard Bethge, *Dietrich Bonhoeffer*, E.T., Collins, London 1967, p. 242.
3. *Die Eiche*, 1933, pp. 368 ff.
4. *Ibid.*
5. Dietrich Bonhoeffer, from *Gesammelte Schriften*, E.T., in *No Rusty Swords*, ed. Edwin Robertson, Collins, London, 1965, p. 251.
6. Eberhard Bethge, *op. cit.*, p. 244.
7. *Ibid.*, p. 244.
8. *No Rusty Swords*, p. 251.
9. *Ibid.*, p. 253.
10. Dietrich Bonhoeffer, *The Cost of Discipleship*, SCM Press, London, 1959, p. 7.
11. *Gesammelte Schriften*, Vol. I, p. 39 (Letter dated 28th April 1934).
12. Eberhard Bethge, *op. cit.*, pp. 289–91.
13. *No Rusty Swords*, pp. 254–5.
14. *Gesammelte Schriften*, Vol. I, pp. 187–89.
15. *Ibid.*, pp. 192–3.
16. *Ibid.*, p. 194.
17. Quoted in full in Edwin Robertson, *Christians against Hitler*, SCM Press, London, 1962, pp. 48–52.
18. Eberhard Bethge, *op. cit.*, p. 298.
19. Klaus Scholder, *The Churches and the Third Reich*, Volume Two: The Year of Disillusionment, Barmen and Rome, SCM Press, London, 1988.
20. G. K. A. Bell, *The Kingship of Christ*, Penguin Books, London, 1954, pp. 30–31.
21. *No Rusty Swords*, *op. cit.*, pp. 285–87.
22. *The Kingship of Christ*, *op. cit.*, p. 26.
23. Klaus Scholder, *op. cit.*, Vol. II, p. 264.
24. *No Rusty Swords*, *op. cit.*, p. 273.
25. *Ibid.*, p. 281.
26. Eberhard Bethge, *op. cit.*, pp. 329–332.
27. G. K. A. Bell, *Christianity and World Order*, Penguin Books, London, 1940, pp. 20–28.
28. Klaus Scholder, *op. cit.*, Vol. II, pp. 263 ff, cf. a lively account in Kenneth Slack, *George Bell*, SCM Press, London 1971, pp. 68–9.

4 The Refugees from Hitler's Germany

Jewish refugees from Germany arrived very early in England as actions taken against them by the Nazis were prohibitive of normal life in their own country. World Jewry quickly rallied to protect its own. But very soon, the Nazi anti-Jewish laws were extended to those of remote Jewish ancestry. Many were Christians and some Christian pastors. They were referred to as "Non-Aryan Christians". These were George Bell's special care, because it was with such difficulty that he managed, very slowly, to rally the Christian churches to their support. When Jews contributed millions for the relief of their fellow Jews, the churches debated long before they contributed as much as £5,000! Indignation was freely expressed, but Bell had little support at first for practical help.

Persistently, George Bell worked for the victims of Nazi brutality and English folly. The long years he worked for these refugees were deeply appreciated by those who had no voice to speak for themselves. After the war, one of their number, an Austrian sculptor, fashioned a statue of St. Michael, who seemed to him to embody the spirit of George Bell. It found a home in the entrance porch to a new church at Harrow Weald dedicated to St. Michael and All Angels. The church was consecrated in 1958, about the time of Bell's death, and it had an inscription written by those who had been refugees, describing the statue as "a thankoffering by men and women who found in Britain a refuge from tyranny in the fourth and fifth decades of the twentieth century after Christ, and as a tribute to George Kennedy Allen Bell, who during his occupancy of the See of Chichester was tireless in his actions on their behalf."[1]

Voices of Protest

Bell was not the only one to speak against the anti-Semitic actions of the Nazis. The fraternity of physicians were ready particularly in Scotland to help their fellows settle down and practise in Britain and elsewhere. Jewish doctors were among Hitler's first targets. As early as 22nd April 1933, restrictions were placed upon many doctors who were employed in the National Health Service in Germany and those restrictions were extended to virtual prohibition to practise at all. Those who came to Scotland were eventually given the opportunity to obtain qualifications which could be registered in Britain, allowing them to practise anywhere in the British Commonwealth.[2] These were Jewish doctors; later other professionals were sometimes enabled to start life afresh in Britain, or the USA, or in Palestine. The majority of non-Aryan Christians were not so fortunate.

On April 7th 1933, the *Jewish Chronicle* appealed to the leaders of the British churches to raise their voices against the inhuman treatment of Jews in Germany. The appeal was heard. Richard Downey, the Roman Catholic Archbishop of Liverpool, responded first of all and at a public meeting declared that "the friends of Germany, those who wish her well, are anxiously watching her to see if they can discern any symptoms of a change of heart". Almost immediately after, Cosmo Lang, Archbishop of Canterbury, appealed to Hitler and his government to restrain the vehemence of their followers. A speaker on behalf of the Free Churches, at the same meeting, professed indignation at evidence of the violation of civic and religious freedom. A Catholic layman, after expressing admiration for much that had been achieved by Hitler, advocated telling the *Führer* very respectfully but very firmly that acts of injustice to the Jews and others would cause the collapse of his regime.

At the General Assembly of the Church of Scotland there was issued in 1934 the first of what became annual statements denouncing anti-Semitism. The *Methodist Recorder* pointed out that there were Christians in Germany who had hitherto been almost unaware of the semitic strain in their blood, who were now deprived of all civic rights.

William Temple, then Archbishop of York, in May 1933 called for an understanding of the cause and character of National Socialism which, as he claimed, had gained the support of a large number of the best citizens of Germany. But whatever excuse, he added, might be made for deeds of violence committed in the course of revolution, no condemnation could be too severe for the persecution and the organised terror which had undeniably ensued. At a later meeting, he insisted that such systematic bullying had taken place in Germany of Jews that silence was forbidden.

Arthur Headlam, Bishop of Gloucester, performed a unique feat in his diocesan newsletter in the summer of 1933 by simultaneously condemning the foolish and violent treatment of the Jews in Germany, and launching his own attack on many of them as constituting an unpleasant and unhealthy alien element within German society, and he imputed to them a measure of responsibility for the violence of Russian Communism and for using their free-thinking Judaism as the basis for an attack upon the Christian faith.

The *Catholic Times* emphasised that the extermination of the Jews was a main plank in the Nazi programme, but a fortnight later condemned international Jewry for the present state of the world distress. It propagated irreligion and immodesty and was in a sinister way behind the world-wide persecution of Catholics. It even went so far as to say that while not condoning the persecution of the Jews as individuals, international Jewry had to be regarded as a "heinous thing, the stamping out of which would be beneficial". The *Catholic Herald* pointed out that all this fuss about the persecution of Jews often meant forgetting the millions of Catholics being persecuted under anti-God and Communist regimes.

> "We do not assail Fascist Italy and applaud Soviet Russia as do some of our loud-voiced and hypocritical contemporaries, to whom wholesale murder and incendiarism in Spain are of no consequence – as they are anti-Catholic – while far lesser wrongs done in Germany are most infamous because done against Jews."

These were the ambiguous protests that formed the background to Christian opinion in the early days of Nazi persecution of the Jews. Gradually the protests grew stronger. By 1936 few could argue in favour of the Nazi treatment although some excused it still.[3]

The majority were horrified by what was happening and the attitude to Jewish refugees from Hitler's Germany grew more sympathetic and more helpful. Bell eventually found much more support for his views. This is illustrated by the attitude towards the celebrations of the 550th anniversary of Heidelberg University. On 28th January 1936 Hensley Henson, Bishop of Durham, heard that British Universities were invited to the celebrations but he had also heard that Heidelberg had been obliged to expel all its Jewish professors and refuse admission to Jewish students. He was furious and said so to George Bell, who thought *The Times* was the place to say so. Bell fired his rocket on 4th February with the key sentence reading:

> "It cannot be right that the Universities of Great Britain, which we treasure, as the very citadel of sound learning, because they are the vigilant guardians of intellectual freedom, should openly fraternise with the avowed and shameless enemies of both."[4]

As a result of this and other protests, no British universities sent representatives to the Heidelberg celebrations.

The Nuremberg Laws 1935

There were verbal protests, however ambiguous at times, but what was needed was real help for the victims. Many had come to Britain and those who were non-Aryan Christians were often in the worst plight. They had come with nothing and they were not the responsibility of the caring Jewish community. The Jewish refugees began to arrive in April 1933. By October the League of Nations appointed James McDonald, an American, High Commissioner for Refugees. The Director of the Commission was Norman Bentwich, a Law Professor at the Hebrew University at

Jerusalem. His wife drew Bell's attention to the refugees of mixed blood who had no claim on the Jewish community to which they did not belong. Bell asked for details and raised the issue at the meeting of the Executive Committee of the Universal Council for Life and Work which met shortly after in Novi Sad. As we have seen[5] this Committee not only pledged support for relief work among these refugees but instructed Bell as chairman to write to the National Bishop, Ludwig Müller, about the Aryan Laws.

George Bell had his strategy as he tried to influence the government in Germany by direct approach and also by raising public opinion against what was happening in Germany. This was a delicate balance of two policies. The more he tried to influence Germany, the less he wanted to arouse hostility towards it. Yet, only by pointing out the gravity of the situation could he possibly obtain help for the refugees. This came to a head with the passing of the Nuremberg Laws on 15th September 1935. These defined most clearly the inferior status of any 'citizen' who had the slightest trace of Jewish blood, even going back to 1815.

Most of the religious press failed to take the Nuremberg Laws seriously, except the now sadly defunct Anglican paper called *Guardian*. The editor rightly saw these laws as being aimed at the extinction of Jewish life in Germany in "relentless, deadly and pitiless destruction". The editor also pointed out, what most papers had missed, that this was carried out in total disregard of world opinion. He then added with great perception:

> "Worst of all would be the loss of Germany's own soul if the exercise proved successful, and there were no more Jews left to persecute, the evil spirit would seek other victims to devour, and turn to other forms of persecution. European Christians were looking on with shame and dread."[6]

That was published in the issue for 15th November 1935. Within five days, George Bell was proposing a cautiously worded resolution at the autumn meetings of the Church Assembly. It expressed sympathy with persecuted Jews in Germany and expressed the hope that Christians in Britain and elsewhere would make it plain to the rulers in Germany that continuance of their repressive policy would arouse indignation and jeopardise confident relations. The resolution was mild enough and hedged with appreciation for what Germany was doing in other areas of national life. It was ably seconded by the Bishop of Southwark.

Despite its caution it was opposed as being "purely political". But that opposition roused Hensley Henson, the Bishop of Durham, to add his weight to the support. His oratory was always worth a score of votes. He had three points to make, he said. Nazi Germany through its treatment of the Jews was in peril of excluding itself from the fellowship of civilised people. The nonsense about race, as if it were some particular poison in the ancestry of Judaism to be guarded against by all manner of restrictions, was sheer hallucination. It was preposterous that the 'Children of Christendom' with such a basic obligation to the Jewish people should turn on the ancient People of God to whom they owed religiously, spiritually and morally almost everything they valued. Then Henson added that, on learning of one base device added to another to degrade, injure and finally destroy the Jew, he felt a kind of blind rage within himself, that they could not draw the sword and go to the help of the low against the mighty.[7]

George Bell could not possibly have approved of that last point and he had been careful not to make a belligerent speech. But it roused the Assembly and the resolution was passed. The London correspondent of a German paper (*Völkische Beobachter*) fastened on this speech as an incitement to war and told the 'English High Church' to mind its own business and look to shootings in Belfast, the plight of the Welsh miners and the squalor of London suburbs. But to the British community of Jews, Hensley Henson was a hero and his speech was circulated in pamphlet form in Germany. This was the last thing George Bell wanted. But the two kept in touch and despite different temperaments were colleagues in the warfare against anti-Semitism.

Practical Help

Meanwhile, George Bell continued his dogged persistence in trying to rouse a practical interest in help for the victims. British public opinion was inclined to regard this plight as a Jewish affair and the churches tended to feel that while this was a humanitarian cause it was not specifically a church cause. The Nuremberg Laws changed this for those who understood that they highlighted the plight of Christian Jews. At last, on 1st May 1936, at the instigation of George Bell, the Archbishop of Canterbury launched a National Christian Appeal for £50,000 for the support of 'non-Aryan' Christian refugees, 2,500 of whom were reckoned to be in actual destitution. George Bell found a supporter in the Revd. W. W. Simpson, later the General Secretary of the Council of Christians and Jews. In June Simpson backed the Archbishop's appeal with an article in the *Church Times*. He drew attention to the parlous plight of Christian men and women of partial Jewish origin accepted on sufferance in Britain and elsewhere, whose future was without hope unless supported by other Christians. He quoted one Jewish refugee as saying:

"We Jews know why we are being persecuted and as a people are accustomed to it. These others do not understand. Why don't you Christians do something practical to help them?"[8]

George Bell consistently protested, and wherever possible face to face with German officials. As things got worse, he began to realise that protests had less and less effect. There was a need for action. The National Christian Appeal had faltered and Bell formed a Church of England Committee for 'non-Aryan' Christians which continued in being until 1945.

The *Paulusbund*

Towards the end of January 1937, Bell visited Berlin to confer with leaders of the Evangelical Church and there discovered something of the work of the *Paulusbund* headed by Dr. Spiero. This was an organisation set up by non-Aryan or Jewish Christians for self-help. In the collection of Bell papers in the Lambeth Palace Library, there is a letter preserved which talks of this visit. After some reference to his visit and to the non-Aryan representatives he met, naming in particular Dr. Spiero and Miss Friedenthal of the *Paulusbund*, Bell adds:

"These were obviously the people who were most representative. They gave me an immense amount of information about the present situation, though I do not think their names ought to be mentioned as having given the information . . . for they were most anxious not to be overheard when they were in my room."

Of the non-Aryan Christians, he says:

"There is no future for them in Germany . . . and it is for the growing generation that their chief concern exists . . . They were grateful for the steps that were being taken for them by the Inter-Aid Committee in London which has received some forty children for placing in English schools (they said they could have sent four hundred easily enough) . . .

"It was really heartbreaking to listen to what they told me without any reserve, and I longed to be able to help them. I feel that I must tell people about the situation as I saw it and try and discover what can possibly be done, even in a small way."

He was encouraged by the existence of the *Paulusbund* and greatly impressed by its representatives, commenting that,

"there would be the nucleus of an organisation if it did so happen that funds were forthcoming. I think there probably are a good many non-Aryan Christians in Germany who are not associated with the *Paulusbund* and I get the impression from the Quakers in London, and also from the Quakers in Berlin, that there were many non-Aryan Christians who felt that they must be very careful indeed as to their relations with foreigners and that they might be often embarrassed by being known to be talking with foreigners about their troubles . . . I am extremely glad that I went."[9]

That letter only adds to the poignancy of the failure of the National Christian Appeal, but of course George Bell did not give up.

At the Church Assembly in June 1938, he raised the issue of the suffering in Germany and Austria. He insisted that he was not being political or attacking the "leadership of the great German State". His plea was to the British Government to do all it could to assist in the emigration of those in such great distress and to invite Christians everywhere to give evidence of their Christian fellowship. He expressed his view that it would be wrong to make a separation and leave Jews to Jews, and Christians to Christians. It was an appeal to all humanity. But he pointed out that, except for the wonderful contribution of the Quakers and some individuals, the Christian response had been woefully small.

Humanity and the Refugees

The year 1938 was a very serious one for those of non-Aryan descent. The *Paulusbund* was not banned, but already in the previous year its activities had been severely restricted by limiting its help to non-Aryans who had no more than fifty per cent Jewish blood. Before speaking to the Church Assembly in June 1938, and despite the fact that he was a marked man by the Nazis, Bell visited Germany again and acquainted himself with the actual situation. This was in April and under the auspices, and, one hoped, the protection of the Life and Work Conference. Germany needed foreign currency and both the *Paulusbund* and George Bell were probably allowed to act because they brought foreign currency into Germany. He also sent his sister-in-law to Hamburg and Berlin to see if an organisation could be set up to care for those eliminated from the *Paulusbund*. In all his speeches Bell made doubly sure that he was well informed, either by personal visits or by acquaintances whose integrity he trusted. Despite the dangers, Bonhoeffer remained in touch with him and visited him in England until the outbreak of war.

On 27th July 1938, Bell made his maiden speech in the House of Lords. It was an urgent appeal to the government to do more for refugees from Germany. He quoted the example of America and pointed out that Britain with its Empire covering so much of the globe could find homes for the young people of Jewish descent who had no future at all in Germany.

His plan was to train young people for work in the Colonies. Bell's major concern was for the young, a new generation who he believed would enrich the life of the British Empire. His appeal was humanitarian, but he did not miss the chance to imply a measure of enlightened self-interest. No one wanted war and Bell least of all. He supported every effort for negotiation. He tempered his attacks on Germany with an admiration for the German people and a surprise that a people so akin to us should act in this way. His concern was not to castigate Germany but to rescue the persecuted. Many German officials whom he had met asked, "What business is it of other countries like England what Germany does with its own people?" His answer was always, "It is our business because we are human beings. If humanity means anything it is impossible to shut our eyes. It is equally impossible to refuse to take action".[10] He was assured that the government would do what it could, but it did precious little. In 1938, the main concern was to pacify Hitler by sacrificing the border territory of Czechoslovakia (Sudetenland) and hence the whole country. These actions, not overtly criticised by Bell, were to aggravate the refugee problem by increasing the number of Jews and other non-Aryans under Nazi control. The annexation of Austria in March 1938 had already brought hundreds of thousands of non-Aryan Christians into the category of potential refugees. The annexation of Sudetenland added to this in October.

On the 7th November, an assassination attempt was made on the German Ambassador in Paris, which misfired and killed Ernst von Rath, a secretary in the German Embassy. The assassin was a young student living in Paris who had heard that his parents were among the Jews who had been expelled from Germany. The student, Herschel Grynzpan, set off a train of hatred against all Jews in Germany, which was not discouraged by the authorities. In fact, Goebbels directed the press to identify all Jews in Germany with the crime. The result was *Kristallnacht*, a fearful pogrom nationwide. Jews were hunted out of their houses, their shops were smashed and looted, their synagogues desecrated and burnt. Thousands of Jews were taken to concentration camps because they were Jews. World opinion was roused and it became easier to find refuge for children of Jewish or part-Jewish parents.[11] Bell's appeal for humanity was more readily heard when it was seen that he was not exaggerating.

George Bell's work for the refugees earned him a doctorate in St. Andrew's University and an invitation to give the Fifth Lucien Wolf Memorial Lecture on 1st February 1939. The lecture was instituted by the Jewish Historical Society in memory of Lucien Wolf (1857–1930), its founder and seven times its president. Lucien Wolf was a great Jewish scholar and Bell had no difficulty in fitting his theme to the interests of the great man. Bell spoke of 'Humanity and the Refugees' and reminded his audience, including the Chief Rabbi in the chair, that Lucien Wolf had been a leading member of the Jewish delegation at the Paris Peace Conference and had taken a successful stand to secure the rights of minorities in Poland and other States. He claimed a oneness with his audience, which was mainly Jewish, by appealing to humanity. After a survey of the historical plight of refugees through the ages, he came to the main purpose of his lecture – 'the refugees, potential and actual, from Germany'.[12]

The Right to Interfere

The policy of the League of Nations at this time was strongly against interfering in the internal affairs of a sovereign nation. However, Bell showed that from Grotius to President Harrison, the right of interference had been maintained in circumstances where human rights were violated.

> "If a tyrant practises towards his subjects, that which no just man can approve, the right of human social connection is not cut off in such a case"
> (Grotius, early seventeenth century).

> "This government cannot be a tacit party to such international wrong. It is constrained to protest against the treatment to which the Jews of Rumania are subjected, not alone because it has unimpeachable ground to remonstrate against the resultant injury to itself, but in the name of humanity"
> (1902, Secretary of State, John Hay, describing the physical and moral oppression which sent the Jews of Rumania as refugees to the USA).

> "A decree to leave one country is, in the nature of things, an order to enter another – some other. This consideration as well as the suggestions of humanity furnishes ample ground for the remonstrances which we have presented to Russia"
> (1891, President Harrison in reference to the Jews from Russia).

George Bell's lecture was an appeal for the refugees from Germany, urging people not only to receive them, but to alter conditions in Germany. He did not speak as a statesman. There were many to remind him of that. But he did speak as a sensitive human being and addressed the Chief Rabbi "as a fellow minister of religion, who feels the plight of the refugees upon his conscience". He continued with his irrepressible optimism to assert his belief that if the national conscience and the conscience of other nations could be aroused, the statesmen of the world would be able to find a solution.

He challenged those who thought we could not take any more refugees, giving examples of other countries who had done far more than Britain. He had done his homework and quoted the offical figures.

> "In France apart from the Spaniards now pouring in, they already have 250,000 refugees, including 40,000 Jews. In Switzerland, with a population of five million, there are 15,000. In England until the other day, there were only 11,000 German refugees".[13]

He argued that the employment of skilled refugees in England had shown that they had provided work for their own people and reduced unemployment.

But once again Bell pleaded for the absorption of German refugees in the Dominions and Colonies, mentioning in particular Palestine, Northern Rhodesia, other countries in Africa, Australia and New Zealand and especially Canada. He pointed out the prosperity which these refugees had in the past brought to their host country. He was able to point to the machinery available for dealing with this massive and growing problem, in particular the inter-governmental Committee set up in Evian, France in July 1938. The need was no longer for machinery but for action. He recognised that the government was concerned with other matters of profound importance for the preservation of peace, but insisted that the refugee problem was inextricably bound up with the problem of peace. His lecture ended on a high note and it had considerable effect:

> "Prime Ministers and their cabinets cannot afford to be passive here; for it is an essential part of the whole business of creating a true international order. The problem of the refugees is a political and an economic problem which cannot be solved unless the governments are determined that it shall be. It is a task which requires generosity and courage and insight in the Heads of Government and their advisers in the New World and in the Old. It is a task the proper handling of which will make all the difference not only to men and women living today, but to posterity. For the problem of the refugee is the problem also of humanity."[14]

In 1939, with Europe on the brink of war, Bell was wiser than the politicians. For he realised that to concentrate solely upon the prevention of war, whilst ignoring the human problem of the plight of the Jewish refugees, spelt disaster. And the result of separating these two issues was, as he feared, not only the failure to prevent war, but also an increase in the suffering of the Jewish people in Germany – and not only Jews!

The failure of the British people and their government to help save Jewish and 'non-Aryan' people until it was too late gave us a share in the guilt of the Holocaust. When we did go to war, it was not for the liberation of the Jewish people but for political reasons, separated from the problems of humanity. Thus we were not only powerless to prevent the Holocaust, but also paid a heavy price in the war which brought a period of British history to a close.

The Second World War

In the months that followed the Lucien Wolf Lecture, George Bell worked incessantly to prevent the outbreak of war. He used every influence he had in the House of Lords, in the Assemblies of the Church and in committees. He did not hesitate to go into print and he kept closely in contact with his German friends. At times he must have seemed a little like Jeremiah to the statesmen and church leaders who, while they wanted to avoid war, had other political intentions than justice and peace. The clearest statement of Bell's attitude to war was in fact published after the war had broken out, although mostly written in those tormenting days when he was trying to avoid it. The publication was a small book called *Christianity and World Order* and the key chapter is Chapter VII "Christianity and War".[15] He begins with a statement of his consistent view that there is no greater contradiction than that between the teaching of Christ and war. He can understand those who say that the supreme Christian aim is 'justice' not 'peace'. "It is better", he says, "to say that the Christian seeks Order; peace being (as S. Augustine said) 'the tranquillity which springs from Order'. And by 'Order' is meant 'a system of right relations'."[16]

He is impatient with those whose constant affirmation is that they want peace. Nobody wants war for its own sake and it was Hitler, as late as 1937, who talked of 'peace' as 'our dearest treasure'. Peace in itself is a meaningless thing as Lenin observed long ago. Peace is only of value when it is seen as the common interest of humanity. With this attitude he examined the European peace movements critically:

> "It is part of the pathos of the immense movement in favour of peace in many European countries, that their Governments have failed to understand the things 'that belong to their peace', by failing to recognise the legitimate needs of others. It is part of the tragedy in which we are involved that the British and other Great Powers could not bring themselves to see that peace as dependent on Order, must be costly to them; and that a sincere devotion to peace involves a sharing of goods, and a

redistribution of possessions, so as to secure right relations between all the Powers."[17]

It goes without saying that Bell had no brief for Hitler, but he regretted the inability of the Allied Powers to see the injustice of the Versailles Treaty. As he said many years before in his ceaseless work for Peace, nations should be compelled to negotiate before going to war. To the last moment he wanted this negotiation with Hitler. He saw Hitler's strategy to get all he could without war, but prepared even 'to put up with war' to obtain the cancellation of the Versailles Treaty; the territories of Czechoslovakia, Poland and Danzig; Germany for all the Germans; iron ore and raw materials; colonies and a world empire. Of course, Bell did not approve of this argument but he quotes a telling appeal by Hitler to Daladier as late as August 27th 1939:

"I therefore year by year sought to obtain, by means of negotiation, the revision of at least the most incredible and most intolerable clauses of this diktat [the Versailles Treaty]. I found this impossible. That this revision ought to take place many far-seeing people in all countries considered to be obvious. Whatever reproaches might be levelled at my methods, however much you might feel obliged to oppose them, no one has the right to overlook or to deny that, thanks to them, it has been possible, in numerous cases, without fresh shedding of blood, not only to find a solution satisfactory for Germany, but also that, by such methods, the statesmen of other countries have been freed from the obligation (which it was often impossible for them to fulfil) of assuming before their own people the responsibility for this revision. For, in any case, it is a point upon which Your Excellency will agree with me; the revision was inevitable. The diktat of Versailles was intolerable."[18]

There was a measure of truth in this argument, however objectionable it may read to us. The statesmen of the day knew that the Versailles Treaty was unjust and had to be revised, but few of them had the courage to face their electorate if they were being 'soft on Germany'. As early as November 1933, a report of a meeting of the World Alliance included a comment by Miles H. Krumbine of Cleveland to the effect that Lloyd George had said to him a long time ago "that when the peace-makers met at Versailles and concocted that witches brew of bitterness, despair and strife, they not only did not intend concocting such a poisonous liquor, but actually intended to be much more moderate; they were as a matter of fact compelled, coerced by the passions of the people back home, into a treaty of violence out of all proportion to their desire".[19]

Apart from the obvious injustice of the Treaty, matters were made a great deal easier for Hitler to break its terms, because the Allies did not keep their promises. The disarmament of Germany was conditional upon a general disarmament and the Geneva Disarmament Conference at which the Allies were to reduce armaments in order to remove the threat to any one country (including Germany) dragged on and did little more than "measure swords around the table".

A Just War?

Hitler had got away with too much on such a pretext and his final threat was, as Bell said, "a terrible weapon to use, a criminal threat".[20] Hitler was surprised that the Allies should in fact go to war because of his proposal to make a 'bloodless conquest' of Poland. But they did. And as it turned out, the conquest was not 'bloodless' for Poland or Germany.

Whether Britain was right or not to declare a state of war with Germany, Bell was uneasy. He asked himself whether, given the potential for destruction of modern methods of warfare, it was ever possible to entertain the idea of a 'just war'.

Using the text, 'A Code of International Ethics', issued from the Catholic University of Louvain by the International Union of Social Studies, he quoted the conditions which Catholic theologians and moralists have consistently maintained for a war to be lawful:

It must be,

(a) declared by a legitimate authority;
(b) have a just and grave cause, proportioned to the evils it brings about;
(c) only be undertaken after all means of peaceful solution of the conflict have been exhaused without success;
(d) have serious chances of success;
(e) be carried out with a right intention.

He noted that the Code adds, "It is also necessary that *moderation* should characterise the conducting of hostilities and should keep the demands of the victor within the limits of justice and charity".[21]

All this was remembered by Bell throughout the war, which he constantly stressed should be conducted with moderation, and more than once, pointed out the need to "keep the demands of the victor within the limits of justice and charity".

Both justice and charity had been violated in the First World War – the use of poison gas, the bombing of non-military targets, and so on – and

George Bell saw the role of the Church to be that of moral compulsion to remember the restrictions imposed by the concept of a 'just war'.

He knew from the beginning that it would be exceedingly difficult for any modern war to satisfy these conditions. At the end when the atomic bomb was dropped first on Hiroshima and then on Nagasaki, he declared that a just war was no longer possible. He had already reached that conclusion in his own mind with the terror bombing of Dresden.

His second question, whether a Christian ought to fight, he left to the individual who had a complex moral decision to make. He did, however, in 1940, consider that it was right that "the overwhelming majority of the young men of the British Empire will back their conviction by fighting with the forces".[22] This he regarded as an existential decision, largely concluded because of the awful consequences of a victory by Hitler. It did not lead him to approve of war, only that Christians ought to do their utmost to defeat the Führer, whose victory "would be so disastrous morally and spiritually for the world". This he said without lessening his conviction that "war itself is the fruit of sin".

George Bell's attitude to war is clearly expressed in the statement of the Oxford Conference on Church, Community and State (1937). He quotes the relevant passage from the Conference Message in the book he was writing as France fell to the German armies:

> "In consonance with its nature as true community, the Church will call the nations to order their lives as members of the one family of God. The Universal Church, surveying the nations of the world, in every one of which it is now planted and rooted, must pronounce a condemnation of war unqualified and unrestricted. War can occur only as a fruit and manifestation of sin. The truth is unaffected by any question of what may be the duty of a nation which has to choose between entry upon war and a course which it believes to be a betrayal of right, or what may be the duty of a Christian citizen whose country is involved in war. The condemnation of war stands, and also the obligation to seek the way of freeing mankind from its physical, moral and spiritual ravages. If war breaks out, then pre-eminently the Church must manifestly be the Church, still united as the one Body of Christ, though the nations where it is planted fight each other, consciously offering the same prayers that God's name may be hallowed, His Kingdom come, and His will be done in both, or all, the warring nations. This fellowship of prayer must at all costs remain unbroken. The Church must also hold together in one spiritual fellowship those

of its members who take different views concerning their duty as Christian citizens in time of war."[23]

Notes

1. R. C. D. Jasper, *George Bell*, OUP, 1967, p. 163.
2. Kenneth E. Collins in *Remembering for the Future*, papers presented at an International Scholars' Conference, Oxford, 10th–13th July, 1988, Theme I, Pergamon Press, Oxford and New York, 1988, pp. 283–296.
3. Richard Gutteridge in *Remembering for the Future*, pp. 352–362.
4. *Ibid.*, pp. 354–355.
5. Cf. pp. 25–6 and 29–30 above.
6. *Guardian* (a church paper founded in 1846, ceased publication 1951) 15th November 1935.
7. *Jewish Chronicle*, 6th December 1935.
8. *The Church Times*, 26th June 1936.
9. *The Bell Papers*, Lambeth Palace Library, Vol. 28, ff. 198–200, cf Jasper, *op. cit.*, pp. 138–9.
10. G. K. A. Bell, *Humanity and the Refugees* (Fifth Lucien Wolf Memorial Lecture), University College, London, 1939, p. 21.
11. Wilfred Harrison, *Rescuers Speaking*, dramatic presentation of many who sheltered Jewish children in Europe at the risk of their lives.
12. G. K. A. Bell, *Humanity and the Refugees*, p. 21.
13. *Ibid.*, p. 24.
14. *Ibid.*, pp. 28–29.
15. *Op. cit.*, pp. 73–87.
16. *Ibid.*, p. 73.
17. *Ibid.*, p. 75.
18. *Ibid.*, pp. 75–76 (Quoted from *The French Yellow Book*, p. 284).
19. Miles H. Krumbine, *World Alliance Newsletter*, November 1933.
20. *Christianity and World Order*, p. 76.
21. *Ibid.*, p. 80 (from *A Code of International Ethics*, Catholic Social Guild, pp. 72–73).
22. *Ibid.*, p. 84.
23. *Ibid.*, pp. 84–85 (from *The Churches Survey their Task*, part of the Message to the Christian Churches, issued by the Oxford Conference in July 1937, p. 59).

5 A Very Special Refugee

Among the thousands of refugees from Germany who left because they had been labelled 'non-Aryans', and therefore marked out for discrimination, was a brilliant constitutional lawyer, called Gerhard Leibholz. At first, Bell's interest was personal, for Gerhard Liebholz was married to Sabine Bonhoeffer (Dietrich's twin sister). They were married on 6th April 1926 in the style of the period, so beautifully described by Sabine herself in her book about the family.[1] The wedding was a traditional upper middle class wedding of families who respected all the customs of the past. It was happy and almost unaware of the fatal background of Germany's fragile democracy and the looming power of National Socialism. It hardly seemed necessary at that time to mention that Gerhard was of Jewish stock – his father was a Jew. After the marriage they continued to live in Berlin and enlarged their circle of friends as Gerhard progressed from being a judge in the district court to *Referent* in the Institute for Foreign Constitutional and International Law. Their first child was born on 30th June 1927 and not long afterwards, Gerhard's important book *On the Problem of Fascist Constitutional Law* was published. He was by then head of the Italian Section. This was his second book and he was accepted as a qualified lecturer on Law in the University of Berlin after his inaugural lecture on this subject. He took his lecturer's examination in Berlin in 1928. By now he had two doctorates in law and was well set for a successful career. He obtained his first professorship in the following year – the Chair of Constitutional Law at the University of Greifswald. He was just 28.

Their second child was born in December 1930 and that completed their family – two girls, Marianne and Christiane. It was an idyllic period in their lives and both loved the quiet university town of Greifswald, surrounded by beautiful country. They seemed far from the anti-Semitic atmosphere already darkening Germany as the Nazi Party grew. Trading upon massive unemployment, 'The Nazis' or the *National Socialist German Workers' Party*, to give it its full name, increased its membership of the Reichstag and its power on the streets. Gerhard was well aware as early as 1930 of the threat to himself, as of Jewish origin, and to his country. So far his family was only occasionally made aware of this by incidents of an unpleasant nature. By 1931, he was appointed Professor of Constitutional Law at Göttingen, but accepted it without enthusiasm. He knew that his days were numbered and that there was no future for him in Germany. It was in Göttingen that he and his family experienced the effects of Hitler's seizure of power. After the Reichstag fire of 1933, Hitler assumed dictatorial powers and steps were taken which steadily removed essential basic rights; the freedom of the individual; the right to keep one's correspondence confidential; the inviolability of the home; the freedom of the press; freedom to join associations; freedom to assemble, as well as the security of private property. This loss of freedom affected all in Germany, but was used most cruelly against those of Jewish origin. Gerhard was, of course, supported by his new family the Bonhoeffers, and this was most clearly seen in the readiness with which they cared for the Göttingen house once Gerhard was forced to flee the country with his wife and children. In 1936, Dietrich Bonhoeffer preached the funeral sermon for his (and Sabine's) grandmother. In that sermon he expressed the values of the whole family except perhaps one cousin who refused to shake the preacher's hand:

"The inflexibility of what is right, the free word of a free man, the obligation to stand by a promise once it is made, clarity and sobriety of speech, uprightness and simplicity in public and private life – on these she set her whole heart . . . She could not bear to see these aims held in contempt or to see the violation of another's rights. Thus her last years were clouded by the great grief she endured over the fate of the Jews among our people, a fate she bore and suffered in sympathy with them. She was the product of another time, of another spiritual world – and that world does *not* go down with her into the grave."[2]

It was for those values that Gerhard Leibholz stood and when he had to leave the country, it was not willingly. He was no emigrant, but a refugee who never ceased in his exile to work for the restoration of such values to his native Germany. For George Bell he became an invaluable asset and a good friend.

Leaving Germany

Conditions in Göttingen became intolerable for Gerhard. The family should probably have left earlier – if all they had in mind was their own safety; but Gerhard Leibholz was not the person to run away from danger or to compromise for security's sake. Day by day his position became more dangerous and eventually he was forced to leave. On 9th September 1938, the family drove out of Göttingen in gloriously sunny weather, apparently for holiday. Dietrich Bonhoeffer and his friend Eberhard Bethge joined them in another car and came with them part of the way to the Swiss border, which they crossed without too much difficulty. Then on to Zürich, where the family stayed at an hotel and followed the news from Germany eagerly. Once it was known that all non-Aryans (as defined by the vicious Nuremberg Laws) would have 'J' stamped on their passports, Gerhard Leibholz knew that he could not return to Germany. Sabine sent a telegram to her parents to say that they 'would like to travel further' and within a few days, her sister Ursula arrived in Zürich to take the children back to Berlin and their car back to Göttingen. The reason for returning the car was that its absence would have been noted eventually and questions asked. Gerhard and Sabine went by train across France and then crossed the channel to England.

It was their first time in this country – although they had heard much about it from Dietrich. They had innumerable addresses from him and made their first home quite near his principal church at Forest Hill in South London. Pastor Boeckheler was at that time minister of this church, an old friend of Sabine from university days. He met them on arrival. Gerhard had very little English and Sabine's was better but not perfect. They were glad of help in finding lodgings, which were in a boarding house near to the church. A few days after their arrival came the sickening news of *Kristallnacht*, the Jewish pogrom of the night of the 9th–10th November 1938. Gerhard was troubled personally because his brother, Hans, who had inherited the textile factory in Sommerfeld from his father, and had already been compelled to surrender it to "Aryan hands" was still in Berlin. Hans in fact took refuge that night in the house of a foreign acquaintance and then made his arrangements to leave. Within a short time he was with Gerhard and Sabine in London. His Swiss wife had preceded him to have her child born in Britain, but after that they returned home.

Things grew steadily worse in Germany. Gerhard's brother moved to Holland early enough to take his household with him. Later, when in 1940 the Germans invaded the Netherlands and rounded up Jews to put in concentration camps, Hans Leibholz and his 'Aryan' wife took their own lives.

Meanwhile, both Gerhard and Sabine were under great stress and Sabine in particular missed the children. Before Christmas 1938, however, her parents brought the children as far as Holland, and equipped with trunks of clothes the children came on to London to be with their parents. Obviously better accommodation was needed and the search began.

Hospitality at Chichester

More than once, Dietrich urged Sabine to contact George Bell, because of his close friendship with him and because he knew people who could help Gerhard to find suitable work. It was not long before they were invited to spend a week-end with the Bishop at the Palace in Chichester and to bring the children. The description which Sabine gives of that first week-end tells so much of George Bell and of his understanding of the German situation:

"These were pleasant days. The old palace and the splendid chapel, the fine garden with its well-kept lawns, the walls overgrown with creepers, the great high rooms with their open fireplaces where Mrs. Bell and the Bishop received us so charmingly – everything was quite new to us and very interesting.

When tea was brought we were still alone with our hosts in the drawing-room. The children sang for them the first English Christmas carols they had learned. Evening prayers were held in the chapel as early as six o' clock, and this, too, made a great impression upon the children. Afterwards at dinner there were several more guests. Suddenly I saw before me the face of someone I knew, though it was much altered. It was an acquaintance of my younger days, a neighbour during my early childhood, the son of a lawyer from Grunewald who had subsequently become a lawyer himself. His head was shaved completely bald and he had just been released from a Nazi concentration camp with a warning not to tell what had happened to him. Here he was, still afraid to talk because of the warning, although he was now in Chichester! . . Dinner took place at a long and wonderful table with well-trained servants to attend our needs. After this we reassembled in the drawing-room, where we read 'Anthony and Cleopatra', the various parts being distributed among the company. The beauty of the English language, which is so often contested in Germany, overwhelmed me.

The next morning at seven o' clock, a housemaid knocked and brought us two pretty trays from which emanated a wonderful aroma of morning tea! . . After morning service in the chapel, breakfast was prepared. The Bishop himself handed us our plates of porridge and cream and later bacon and eggs which had been placed hot on the sideboard. Mrs. Bell poured out the tea, a maid brought hot toast and orange marmalade. A huge log fire was blazing in the largest fireplace which I ever saw in England, but even so it was rather cold in that gigantic old dining hall. The conversation turned upon the German Church Struggle, Ecumenism and the problem of finding posts for the refugee pastors."[3]

That whole account of a week-end in Chichester in January 1939 has an air of unreality about it. For that refugee family it seemed like a dream and for Gerhard it was the beginning of a relationship with the kindest man in England and the best informed about German affairs.

The Outbreak of War

The idyllic week-end at Chichester could not go on forever, but the link with George Bell continued and grew as he assessed the value of Gerhard Leibholz and recognised the need for a good legal mind in Britain at that time. It was not easy to find a post for him suitable to his qualifications. George Bell encouraged him and, later, their correspondence became one of the most valuable collections for an understanding of the issues involved in wartime Britain, both legal and humanitarian. But that lay in the future. England was growing tired of Chamberlain's 'appeasement' and as the demonic drama unfolded in Europe, there was a pressure to do something. The Declaration of War on 3rd September 1939 came as an immense relief throughout the country.

Before then, Gerhard and Sabine had been greatly encouraged by visits from Dietrich. When he came, said Sabine, "It was as if we were suddenly upheld by someone. Gerhard and I both felt a great inrush of strength and courage". Dietrich was always an optimist and so much happiness emanated from his strong personality. Times were far from bright and it took all his optimism to paint scenes of hopefulness. There were those who said of him, "The sun rose when he entered the room, because he was able to be unreservedly joyful". One of the things Sabine feared was that once war was declared they would never see him again. She was right. He was with them when the news came through of the death of Pastor Paul Schneider[4] in Buchenwald and it seemed a strange foreboding.

Dietrich was convinced that the boarding house in Forest Hill was quite inadequate and insisted that they move. After a brief visit to the Dutch coast to meet her parents, Gerhard and Sabine needed no persuasion to move to St Leonards, near Hastings, and after a short time in a hotel found a suitable flat, where they were when war was declared. It was near to the sea and not far from an old house that the Bishop of Chichester had rented on his own initiative for forty refugee German pastors. All had been persecuted by the Nazis for their Jewish descent. No pastorates were open to them in Germany. Bell intended to install them in course of time in various parishes in England as curates or vicars. Often their English was poor, but with tireless effort he settled most of them. Canon Griffiths, who was put in charge of these pastors and their families, came to know the Leibholz family well.

Internment

Soon after the declaration of war in 1939, 112 special tribunals were set up to categorise those of 'enemy' nationality. In all, some 74,000 were categorised in three groups:

a) those who were beyond suspicion, which constituted the vast majority; 55,000 were given category 'C' and granted the status of 'refugees from Nazi oppression'. They were exempt from all restrictions other than those normally imposed on foreigners.

b) those held to be less trustworthy and therefore graded 'B' and subject to some limitations.

c) those who appeared to constitute a security risk, graded 'A' and interned at once. There were about a thousand in this category.

There was a growing sympathy for those refugees of Jewish origin, but the categorisation seemed fair and necessary.

For the first six months of the war nothing very much happened. Hitler was hoping to present the Polish affair as a *fait accompli* and avoid a large scale European war. Nothing much more was done about internment until things warmed up in the summer of 1940. Then there appeared to be a threat of invasion. France collapsed, the British Forces evacuated like a defeated army from Dunkirk and Germany was almost master of continental Europe. At first, some 2,000 further refugees who lived in coastal regions, which, because of possible invasion, had been declared Protected Areas, were interned. Then all male category 'B' were interned followed later with internment of the women, as invasion became a real possibility. Broadsheets were issued to every household instructing what to do "If the Invader Comes". There was something of a panic. Churchill said "collar the lot" and all male refugees between 16 and 70, regardless of category were interned. As a rule, police stations served as initial collecting points. Then followed a day or night in a transit camp. From there on, the War Office took over and the internees were transferred to various camps. Those on the Isle of Man were not bad, but others were notorious.

It will be enough to quote from the experience of one refugee in Warth Hill Camp in Lancashire.

> "Conditions in the Warth Hill internment camp in the summer of 1940 were utterly appalling. Warth Hill was a typical Lancashire cotton mill – a huge rectangular brick building, three or four storeys high, with regular rows of large windows, many of which were broken. It stood in its own grounds by a river (water power was still in use) just outside the town of Bury.

When I arrived, Warth Hill had been in operation as an internment camp for just a week or two. First arrivals had a horrendous task, clearing the floors of oily cotton waste, sludge and general filth. We were given coarse canvas palliasses and two blankets and taken to the store to collect straw; we filled the palliasses and joined the throng – row upon row of palliasses stretching the length of the mill floor. We also collected a mess tin each, spoon, knife, fork and a tin mug. A new life had begun. The building held 2,000 people we were told and these were served by twenty taps and basins and twenty latrines.

Food was abominable – one day I remember a large barrel was rolled in – it contained salt herrings. That was our dinner. On questioning this 'meal' we were told by the guards that they thought Germans liked herring. The attitude of our guards – soldiers of the Lancashire Regiment, I believe was understandable though upsetting. The average non-commissioned soldier was not blessed abundantly with knowledge or education; he had been given the job of guarding Germans, and we were at war with Germany, that was all he knew. Who were 'we' anyway?"[5]

The majority were German and Austrian Jews and among the 2,000 there was a very high proportion of professional people – doctors, professors, lawyers and so on.

There was less physical hardship on the Isle of Man, where the 'camps' consisted largely of streets of boarding houses, of which there were several on the island. All internment camps developed a kind of camp culture and there was an extraordinary range of cultural activities and some very well written camp newspapers. At Rushden, in the Midlands, the internees set themselves the task of providing schools and a kindergarten for children who had been deprived of the normal educational facilities.

One of the fears of many internees was that they might be deported. In June and July 1940, over 4,000 internees – German and Italian civilians, German P.O.W.'s, Jewish refugees – were deported to Canada. One of the transport ships, the *Arandora Star* was torpedoed by a German U-boat with 700 drowned. Eight days later the troop-ship *Dunera* carrying (far in excess of her complement) 712 internees including 444 survivors from the *Arandora Star* left Liverpool for Australia. Conditions were shocking during their long voyage and internment at the end of it. It was the darkest chapter in a dark and ugly story. As the news got out, public opinion forced the government to take some measures to improve conditions and reduce the number interned.

Gerhard Leibholz Interned

On Whit Monday, 1940, a policeman appeared at the flat in St. Leonards and in the kindest way told Sabine that he had to take Gerhard into internment. Sabine remained without news of him for many weeks. Some neighbours were most kind and sympathetic. Gerhard met with more spite. One policeman said to him somewhat brusquely, "Now you will have to suffer for your Führer". Gerhard's wit did not leave him, he replied, "Thank you, I have already done that in Germany". On his arrival in England, Gerhard had been examined before the tribunal and designated on his passport as "Refugee from National Socialist Oppression". It was difficult for any of the family to understand why he should now be designated "Enemy Alien". Sabine was packed and ready to move as soon as she knew what was to happen. She waited ten days before there was any word. Despite the danger of remaining on the South coast with the expected invasion, she decided to stay in St. Leonards until she heard from Gerhard about his and their future. She was worried at the news that many 'enemy aliens' were being shipped to Australia and Canada. Gerhard was taken to the Aliens' Internment Camp in Huyton, near Liverpool. The conditions were wretched. No newspapers, no writing or receiving of letters. The uncertainty and especially the fear of being transported to the 'Colonies' led many to deep depression, some attempting and others succeeding in their suicides. As soon as the Bishop heard that Gerhard had been interned he came to visit the family in St. Leonards. He prayed for Gerhard's release and for Dietrich and his brothers. He promised to try to get Gerhard released, but they were difficult times, with the Fall of France and the entry of Italy into the war. Some spoke up in parliament for the victims of Nazi oppression, but the military insisted that, in view of the activity of the Fifth Column in Holland and Belgium, internment was a necessary security measure. The country was divided and the military had their way.

At last, Sabine heard from Gerhard and she immediately prepared to leave St. Leonards. Canon Griffiths had already told her of the widow of a doctor in Devon, a Mrs. Wilkinson, who had a large country house with a glorious garden and she wanted to take in *only* German refugees. It seemed the perfect solution. Sabine and the children left St. Leonards and came by train to Willand in Devon with fourteen trunks; their entire possessions. There, Sabine received letters from Gerhard, while for the children it was a holiday in the beautiful Devon countryside. Mrs. Wilkinson knew about children, for she had had twelve of her own. After some weeks, among the most critical of the war, Willand was declared a restricted area and the family had to move again. Gerhard was still interned and Sabine decided upon Oxford. They stayed at a new boarding house run by Mrs. Harrison who was politically well informed and also understood when Sabine and the two children arrived with so many trunks. The house was let mostly to students, but one room was set aside for Sabine and the two children. Mrs. Harrison refused payment. "I am not charging you anything" she said. "You are refugees." There was no anti-German feeling in her house but Sabine met with some in Oxford. This was natural enough and she does not appear to have suffered much. Life became pleasanter when Gerhard was allowed to write every day although the glazed envelope was always boldly stamped, "Opened by Censor".

Bell's deep Concern

Pastor Hildebrandt, the close friend of Dietrich Bonhoeffer, and one of the non-Aryan refugees, who was also interned, described a visit by the Bishop of Chichester to his internment camp on the Isle of Man. It illustrates the Bishop's deep sense of shock at the conditions and his determination to do something about it:

> "When the Bishop appeared he could scarcely reply to our welcome. He was almost speechless and could only stammer and stutter. It was an unforgettable moment. The sight of the refugees in their new captivity was just too much for him – it was not only a question of a wrong to so many of his personal friends, it was a moral burden on the English people. It was clear to him that something must be done immediately. He listened to what we had to say, and then acted. On returning from the Isle of Man he called on the central postal censorship office in Liverpool, inspected the stacked postbags of the past six or eight weeks for which the internees had waited in vain, and suggested quietly but firmly that the letters might be delivered to the people to whom they were addressed. Three days later the camp post office was inundated."[6]

On 6th August 1940, Bell once again raised the question of the release of these refugees in the House of Lords. He spoke eloquently of the appalling conditions, of gifted men wandering about aimlessly. He clearly defined the difference between aliens of enemy nationality and refugees from the enemy. He asked, "Do you know, my Lords, that in Camp Douglas alone, out of 1,900 internees there are 150 who were in concentration camps in Germany?"

After this, a ray of hope came for the Leibholz family. It was announced that those refugees who could produce a visa for America would be released at once. Dietrich had already suggested to Sabine that if they felt they should leave England, she should write for such a safeguard to his American friends – Niebuhr, Coffin and Lehmann. They responded with an invitation to the family and the offer of a Lectureship for Gerhard. About that time a vessel transporting children to America was torpedoed and they dropped the idea. But meanwhile the Bishop of Chichester had interceded for Gerhard Leibholz. Sabine received a telegram on 26th July 1940: "Hope to be in Oxford at half past six". It was from Gerhard and they met him at the station. In his diary that day there was a one-word entry – RELEASE.

The family settled in Oxford, the children went to school and Gerhard found more congenial company and a promise of suitable work. Lodging was a problem and they had to move six times, but Oxford was clearly the best place for those war years. The Bishop of Chichester visited the family there and built up a close relationship with the children. The Bishop also had news of Dietrich, usually through Visser 't Hooft, the General Secretary of the World Council of Churches in process of formation, whom Dietrich met on his visits to Geneva. Sabine would usually receive a letter from Dietrich whenever he was in a neutral country. Thus a closeness grew up between the Bishop and the Leibholz family, partly due to their common bond of affection for Dietrich. Later it developed into a close consultative relationship with Gerhard Leibholz upon whose judgement Bell increasingly depended and whose expertise he valued.

The Correspondence

In 1974, there was published in Germany a collection of letters between the Bishop of Chichester and Professor Gerhard Leibholz which covered the period from 1939 to 1951. It was given the title, *An der Schwelle zum Gespaltenen Europa*[7] (On the Threshold of a Divided Europe). The earliest letters were much concerned with news of Dietrich, assurances of a readiness to help, suggestions for work and contacts. Then there is rejoicing in Gerhard's release from internment. The first real exchange of views comes in a letter on 12th November 1940, when Gerhard Leibholz wrote to George Bell about his recently published *Christianity and World Order*[8] which Gerhard had just read. He expressed his appreciation and gratitude for the book and also his agreement with the Bishop in his assessment of the present crisis in Europe, approving of the analysis of the conditions under which Europe lived. In particular he underlined the Bishop's insistence that to be a Christian meant to bear witness to the Christian message in the real situation of the world. "It is a fatal mistake to think that you can keep religion separate from public life", he wrote, "although many churches and individuals attempt to do it. Today, the

Church cannot continue to be fragmented or have its proclamation of the Gospel limited. Although that is what the totalitarian states would like to see".

For the greater part of the letter he takes up what Bell says about Secularism. This refers to the second chapter of the book and is a subject which was much discussed during the war in Britain. So much had changed in the inter-war years largely precipitated by the First World War, which provided a kind of watershed between two worlds. Before 1914, Britain looked like a Christian country; in 1940, many of the more evident Christian traits had disappeared from public life. Sunday was secularised and Good Friday was no longer considered a religious day. Bell analysed contemporary literature to describe what was wrong with society, but did not attempt to call for a return to earlier patterns. What he did insist upon was that we should look at the kind of society we were producing. If we object to totalitarian states, what kind of states do we approve of? We cannot answer "Christian" or even "religious", because to all intents and purposes life had become secular. We have not thought clearly enough about what we are doing. Bell ends his chapter with two questions:

1. "What is the conception of morality which can offer us any hope of escape from destruction?"
2. "What is the dynamic and simple faith which may yet save western civilisation before it is too late?"[9]

Gerhard Leibholz's response to this which is the heart of his letter, is:

"The Church must become a political reality . . . For this task it cannot confine itself to one sphere of life. In other words, and as you insist, Christians must derive the ground rules of their faith from real demands and live in a really Christian way as the Gospel requires. We must relate our faith in God daily anew to our faith in our neighbour. I believe that I can remember a comment from the Confessing Church before the outbreak of the war, which said that Christianity was no private affair and does not limit itself to a particular 'part of human life; the Word of God rather claims the whole of human life'.

"The situation today would probably not be so critical if there had been more boldness and less weakness and opportunism in the institutional church. These widespread, general defects apply with particular weight to the present situation and are of wide-ranging significance as in other fields. . . What therefore seems to me to be the more pressing task for the future is 'selection'; i.e. to put the best people in the right places.

"Apart from this, I want to take your argument about modern secularism a great deal further.

"Like you, I am of the opinion that one cannot automatically equate Christian with western civilisation, even if it is on Christian foundations. For in the last resort, the secular character of modern civilisation is responsible for the present situation. It is in the totalitarian, anti-liberal state that it appears to me that the secular process has reached its highest point. That which began in the Renaissance and in Humanism, the Age of Enlightenment, through Natural Law, developed its first high level in Liberal Democracies. It was, therefore, no accident that its success in the emancipation of the *bourgeoisie* in the 18th and 19th centuries together with freedom of thought, led to a conflict with Christianity, and the Christian Church was often the focal point and initiator of actions against the powers of Enlightenment, Rationalism and Humanism. In the present situation we see a much sharper conflict, because the growing Secularism in the totalitarian state puts in question, not only the basis of Christianity, but also that of Humanism, Rationalism and political Liberalism. The secularising of Christian thought, in so far as it was still bound to Christianity, earlier maintained belief in the unity of mankind and the human spirit; but even this decisive faith is shattered by the new radical Secularism, and the growing Materialism of modern thought. For this reason, it can be said that Christianity and modern western civilisation have something in common."[10]

With this letter the two minds synchronised. Leibholz had already written on a similar theme to Visser 't Hooft, probably in relation to a book being written by William Paton on *The Church and the New Order*[11], published in July 1941, but not before it had been commented upon by Dietrich Bonhoeffer and Visser 't Hooft when they were in Geneva together.

Bell's book led Leibholz to think again and he added:

"Now after reading your book, the whole section of mine on the 'International Order of the Future' needs to be rewritten."

For his part Bell replied within a few days that "in a new edition of my book, much of your comment will find a place".

There is little doubt from early correspondence that Bell had a very high regard for Leibholz's work. He quickly found that as he had had an authoritative source on the Church Struggle in Dietrich Bonhoeffer, he now had an expert consultant on legal matters in Gerhard Leibholz. Bell helped Leibholz, both by putting him in touch with people who could invite him to lecture and directly recommending editors to publish his material. But there is equally no doubt that Leibholz was invaluable to Bell. This was evident quite early in the question of the internees. The editor of the *American Journal of International Law* wrote to Gerhard Leibholz early in January 1941 asking to see his essay on "The Internment Policy and the Refugee Problem". He did not publish the article at once in his journal although it did appear in America later. Meanwhile Bell had read this essay and was very greatly impressed. He liked the way Leibholz used good source material and the clarity with which he presented his case. He did everything he could to get this essay published, but Sir Cecil Hurst of the International Court in the Hague thought it inadvisable. This did not prevent Bell from making good use of it for his speeches in the House of Lords.

In the same way he consulted Leibholz when writing his famous letters to *The Times*. Many of the letters between Bell and Leibholz in 1941 deal with their critical attitude to the Atlantic Charter, for example. We shall have cause to look at later correspondence, but it is already clear that Gerhard Leibholz was in Bell's opinion, "a very special refugee".

Notes

1. Sabine Leibholz-Bonhoeffer, *The Bonhoeffers: Portrait of a Family*, Covenant Publications, Chicago, 1994, pp. 56–59.
2. Bonhoeffer, *Predigen, Auslegungen, Meditationen*, Band 2, 1935–1945, Chr. Kaiser Verlag, München, 1985, pp. 48–53.
3. Sabine Leibholz-Bonhoeffer, *op. cit.*, pp. 100–101.
4. *The Pastor of Buchenwald*, edited and translated, E. H. Robertson, SCM Press, London, 1955 (first martyr of the Confessing Church, 1939).
5. AJJ (Association of Jewish Refugees) *Information*, June 1990.
6. Sabine Leibholz-Bonhoeffer, *op. cit.*, pp. 127–128.
7. *An der Schwelle zum Gespaltenen Europa*, correspondence between Bell and Gerhard Leibholz, edited Eberhard Bethge/Ronald Jasper, Kreuz Verlag, Stuttgart and Berlin, 1974.
8. G. K. A. Bell, *op. cit.*
9. *Christianity and World Order*, p. 28.
10. *An der Schwelle zum Gespaltenen Europa*, pp. 18–20.
11. William Paton, *The Church and the New Order*, SCM Press, London, July 1941.

6 The Bishop in Wartime

For twenty years including all the war years, George Bell was an episcopal member of the House of Lords. From the beginning, he took that office seriously and was conscientious both in attendance and in his readiness to speak or take part in debates. He regarded his office as a moral guide to government, not simply as a representative of the Established Church, who might be expected to speak on matters concerning the Church. When moral issues were involved or when the nation was undertaking an enterprise which conflicted with ethical standards derived from the Christian Faith, he spoke out boldly.

At no point did he want this nation to go to war and throughout that war which inevitably came, he sought every means to end it. He confessed he was not a pacifist, but he could not see how war could solve anything without incurring much greater harm to victor and defeated alike. He pleaded for negotiation and even when war was declared he did not give up hope. Once Poland was overrun and Germany seemed reluctant to take any further steps to attack the West, he entered the dangerous game of negotiating to end the war. When that failed he tried to mitigate the harm done to civilians and particularly to women and children. He opposed the bombing of towns, even in retaliation.

The Moral Dilemma

Few were more aware of the evil consequences of Nazi rule, both in Germany and soon spreading over conquered Europe. Bell also knew that there were many in Germany who were opposed to Hitler. He was well informed about the Church struggle to resist the influence of the Nazi perversion of the faith; he had dealt personally with church and secular leaders in Germany; he opposed National Socialism and supported those who wanted to end it. He could not therefore disagree with the war aims of Britain and its Allies to destroy the German government. What he pleaded for was a recognition that Germany and the Nazis were not identical. The Nazis should be deposed, but Germany should neither be destroyed nor enslaved. Many of those who gave wholehearted support to the war depicted the German people and the Nazis as indistinguishable. In *Christianity and World Order*, the Bishop makes his position crystal clear, but it was not so accepted by those who had but one aim – to win the war:

> "Germany and National Socialism are not the same thing. The West can never make terms with the National Socialist

ideology. But the West can make terms with Germany, if only Germany could go through a revolution, such as those which Britain and France have gone through!"[1]

This was not merely an expression of personal opinion. The strength of Bell's position was that he could depend upon a wide range of advisers. His role in the World Council of Churches gave him access at an early stage to draft documents which were circulated widely, discussed and amended.

Thus Visser 't Hooft, who from 1938 was General Secretary of the Provisional Committee for the World Council of Churches (in process of formation), presented him with a memorandum on the West as a democratic tradition – 'that group of nations whose political ideology is characterised by the conviction that the rights of the state should be and are limited by law and therefore practice some form of parliamentary government'.

Bell's reference to Germany as in need of a revolution refers to Visser 't Hooft's further definition of the democratic West as 'nations who have undergone the influence of the revolutions of 1688 (England), 1776 (USA) and 1789 (France)'. The ideologies of these countries differ widely, but they are related to each other in that they all have developed some counterbalance to autocratic power. Bell traces the different development in Germany to the philosophy of Bismarck – 'the only healthy foundation of a great State is its State egoism, and not romanticism'. Bell does not hesitate to criticise the West for its clumsy attempts to impose a democratic constitution after the First World War upon a Germany that felt it to be alien. Germany needed to find its own revolution and Bell believed that there were men who would bring it about. He knew the men and he also knew that they could not do it so easily in wartime when patriotism was at stake and a revolution might look like treason. 'National Socialism', he consistently maintained, 'is not typical of the German spirit. Rather it is a caricature of one strain of the German character'.

Bell lost no opportunity in presenting his views. They were unpopular because war fever was mounting. But he saw his chance during the phoney war, as it was called. After the occupation of Poland, the German forces were quiescent. It seemed to him a time to consider whether the continuance of war was the right procedure. His consistent view was simply that National Socialism had to be destroyed, but not Germany. He advocated a period of peace in which, for all our dislike of Nazism, we could negotiate with Germany and at the same time encourage that German resistance which was widespread in very significant areas of German life: the legal profession, the army, and especially the *Abwehr* (the German office of military intelligence, which for reasons of security required secrecy and was not even open to investigation by the *Gestapo*).

When he failed to convince his peers of the value of negotiation, he urged that the war be conducted with reconstruction in mind at the end. 'One of the most important tasks is the constructive, moral and political effort which should be going on in parallel with the war', he said, making plain that 'the West does not desire to crush Germany'. This alone, he maintained, would encourage the forces of resistance within Germany and make it possible for them to bring about the desired revolution.

The First Hopes of Peace

When Hitler had overrun Poland, but had not moved his forces westward, the sovereigns of two neutral countries, the King of the Belgians and the Queen of the Netherlands, offered to mediate and seek peace. In the House of Lords, the Earl of Darnley welcomed this and Bell supported him. It was important for Bell to declare his credentials. He realised that he would be misunderstood and be labelled as a 'pacifist' and a 'peace at any price' man. He felt like Jeremiah speaking in favour of negotiating with the Babylonians and knew that he might well suffer the same fate! He therefore began with considerable emphasis: 'I am not a pacifist, nor am I one of those who ask that peace should be made at any price'.[2] But he argued that the choice for this nation lay between a fight to the finish which was more heroic and a negotiation which at this stage might be misunderstood as 'appeasement'. The heroic alternative meant such a sacrifice – the inevitable extension of the scope of the war, the moral, physical and spiritual exhaustion of the belligerents, perhaps the collapse of European civilisation – that no effort should be spared in trying honourably to face the other alternative. His speech was well documented. He outlined politically the conditions for stable peace in Europe which meant a careful consideration of frontiers and the recognition of the rights of ethnic groups. This was aimed at reducing friction and should be accompanied by reductions of armaments and reorganisation of international economic relations. Today, that speech makes obvious good sense, but it was spoken after Hitler's ruthless invasion of Poland, when the country was at war. His 'positive, ascertainable, concrete and real guarantees' were up against a bulwark of emotion. His hope that he might say 'this without fear of being misunderstood', was slender, but he affirmed with utter sincerity 'I abhor Hitlerism'.

The end of the speech dealt with the religious and spiritual factor as the most important for keeping the peace of Europe. He added, 'making and keeping the peace will be much more possible now than it would be when the whole world has been overwhelmed with disaster'.

This first intervention in wartime was well received by the foreign press. The Scandinavians, who knew him well, and who had already offered their help in the maintenance of Christian fellowship across the belligerent divide, gave it much publicity. It was front page news in the *New York Times* and reported in several European papers. But the British press virtually ignored it. That speech was made on 13th December 1939, and Bell saw support for it in the Pope's Christmas Eve message with its Five Peace Points. He attached considerable importance to this message as can be seen from the space he gives to it in *Christianity and World Order*.[3] There he quotes the Five Peace Points and summarises them at the end, making the comment, 'I have little doubt that if these five points could be accepted, and if the principles could be applied in the concrete situation, the whole prospect of a new order and of genuine reconstruction would be immensely advanced'. Of course, he recognises, as no doubt the Pope did too, that the details needed to be worked out by historians, economists, politicians and diplomats, but the Five Points provided a basis. Bell also saw in the fifth point an invitation to cooperation which suited his ecumenical spirit.

> "They [peoples and their governments] must be guided by that universal love which is the compendium and most general expression of the Christian ideal and *which therefore may serve as a common ground also for those who have not the blessing of sharing the same faith with us.*"

The italics are Bell's and he comments:

> "To my mind this last expression is in the nature of an invitation to non-Roman Christian leaders to work out together and uphold together the common ground".[4]

Bell went further and suggested the holding of a conference in Rome, presided over by the Pope or his representative, to which the churches of the ecumenical movement would be invited to discuss the Five Peace Points and work out together the common ground and hold it in the name of the Kingdom of God. He had no illusions about the difficulties of reunion with Rome. But he saw this one common ground in the desire to preserve the peace and civilisation of Europe in the name of the Church whose foundations were closely related to the foundations of European culture.

In his New Year (1940) Diocesan Letter, the Bishop expressed the same views.

> "It is our task to make the European tradition, a tradition animated by the Christian spirit, prevail; to interpret its

character, to show it reintegrating a dying civilisation by a rekindling of the old strength at the ancient sources; to set it forth in all its implications derived from an all-embracing Christian faith; and reveal it embodied in the political and economic order, in the relation of nations, and in the collective life, as well as in the experience of the individual personality."[5]

The Vansittart Broadcasts

Bell's first cause in the war was the establishing of the thesis that Germany was a nation with whom we could deal on honourable terms. The reputation of the Nazis, especially in their treatment of the Jews, made that a difficult thesis to maintain. It could only be maintained on the premise that National Socialism was an aberration and not typical of the German people. It was much easier to maintain that Germany was 'at it again'. We had fought a war before with this belligerent people and they were incurably bent upon dominating Europe. We had been too soft the first time, but now they had gone too far again and we must teach them a lesson they cannot forget. They must never be allowed to do it a third time. This thesis carried with it the corollary that all Germans were Nazis. Bell knew this to be untrue and he also saw that while it was believed, there was no hope of a negotiated peace. The wheels were grinding slowly towards 'war to a finish'.

The growing dissatisfaction with Chamberlain the 'appeaser' made Bell's task harder. The agreements made at Munich which Hitler had violated seemed to show that you could not trust the Germans. A negotiated peace now would only be giving them time to recover after the Polish expedition. The country began to demand action and there were calls for Churchill to take over. The phoney war continued and after a period of relief that bombs had not fallen on London in the early stages, the country looked for action. Churchill was recalled to the Admiralty. As First Lord, he was invited to give a speech, a toast to 'England' on St. George's Day 1940. Pressure of work prevented him from making that speech and Duff Cooper made it on his behalf. It was a speech such as Churchill might have made. It attacked the German nation and ridiculed the idea that you could distinguish between Germans and Nazis. The horrors that were happening in Germany were typical of the race. It was a racist speech, attacking Bell's central position, that you could separate Germans from their evil government and encourage them to overthrow it. Duff Cooper talked of the crimes of Europe as the work, not of one man or even of a minority of thugs, but the crimes of a whole nation. Bell's position was described as 'wishful thinking and dangerous'. Whatever part Churchill had in the writing of that speech he did not repudiate it and it certainly echoed a feeling in the country. It was applauded. We were not trying to root out a cancer in the German nation, but Germany was the cancer in the body of Europe.

Bell saw the danger of this line which ran counter to the government's declared policy about the Allied war aims that 'The West does not want to crush Germany'. A few weeks later, Churchill became Prime Minister.

Sir Robert (later, Lord) Vansittart was chief diplomatic adviser to the government and Churchill authorised him to prepare a series of broadcast talks for the BBC Overseas Service. Their overall title was 'Black Record: Germans, Past and Present'. It was an undisguised propaganda exercise, designed to build up hatred against Germany as a nation, particularly in America and the British Commonwealth and Empire. All Germans were criminals of the Hitler type. They were by nature perfidious, brutal, arrogant, lovers of war and haters of liberty. Their nature had not changed since the days of Tacitus. They must be crushed, you cannot reason with them. Unless you beat them to their knees they will be at your throat. It was soap-box stuff of the crudest kind. Bell had lost his first cause. Vansittartism was not accepted by all but it was popular during the war. 'The only good German is a dead one' appeared in slogans and graffiti. Yet Bell did not give up. On 20th January 1941, after Dunkirk and in the midst of the bombing of London, he wrote a letter to *The Sunday Times.* It was a courageous letter, not destined to make him popular with the Londoners who had spent so many nights in air-raid shelters. This was no longer a phoney war. The 'desert rats' were encountering Rommel in North Africa. Hitler had taken France and was dominant in Europe, although he had to conduct his negotiations with Molotov in an air-raid shelter. The war was raging. Britain was hitting back, but alone. Roosevelt talked of making America 'the arsenal of democracy'. The 'Lend-Lease' agreement was being discussed, 'the most unsordid act in history' Churchill called it when Congress passed this life-line to Britain on 8th February 1941. Meanwhile, Hitler was building his Grand Alliance and using bits of the British Empire as bait for Allies. Malta had bravely resisted savage attacks. The nation was in war fever. In this situation, Bell's letter on 20th January urged a 'moral' offensive against Germany. It would need more than a military defeat to restore peace in Europe. What was needed, he said, was for the government to devote more time and energy to moral and spiritual propaganda. He continued to insist that there were still many in Germany, 'silenced by the Gestapo and the machine-gun, who longed for deliverance from a godless Nazi rule'. This phrase was again used in a speech he made in the Stoll Theatre on 10th May, when he took a very firm stand against Vansittartism. He insisted that this good Germany, these silenced and yet active resisters, whom he knew, were equally longing for 'the coming of Christian Order in which they and we can take our part'. With a rhetoric which was not his customary style unless he was deeply moved, he concluded, 'Is no trumpet call to come from England, to awaken them from despair?'[6]

The British public had heard of Pastor Niemöller, but were not persuaded that he represented a substantial number of Germans opposed to the Nazi regime.

The Bombing of Non-Military Objectives

In the early months of the war, all agreed that there would be no 'bombardment from the air of civil populations or unfortified cities', to use the words of President Roosevelt's appeal on 1st September 1939. The situation changed in the Spring of 1940, when it became clear that this was a different war from the First World War – not trench warfare but *Blitzkreig*. Germany was master of Europe and poised to invade England. England's only effective means of striking at the enemy was from the air and the RAF proceeded to bomb the French ports and other targets directly involved in the invasion preparations. After a while other areas were bombed and the mutual bombing of London and Berlin began on the weekend of 25th–26th August 1940. Bell described this as a 'calamitous mistake', and he was supported by more than one military man. Military historians, like Liddell Hart, objected for other reasons. They thought it was absurd to take part in the bombing game when we were so inferior to Germany in bombing power. The Germans were so much better placed to play this game of 'inter-city competition in destruction'. Bell's reasons, however, were moral. Archbishop Davidson had objected to retaliation bombing in the First World War and Bell saw no reason to divert from that stand in the Second.

The destruction of cities by bombing reached horrific proportions when in the Spring of 1941 the Germans systematically destroyed Belgrade. They were to do this pattern-bombing destruction later with other cities, like Rotterdam, but this was the first. It moved the Pope to appeal to all belligerents on Easter Day, 11th April 1941, to place a limit on the sufferings of non-combatants, particularly women and children. Bell followed this up at once with a letter to *The Times* appealing for some limitation of aerial bombardment:

> "It is barbarous to make women and children the deliberate object of attack. . . If Europe is civilised at all, what can excuse the bombing of towns by night and the terrorising of non-combatants who work by day and cannot sleep when darkness comes? . . Is it not possible for the British Government to make

a solemn declaration that they for their part will refrain from night bombing (either altogether or of towns with civilian populations) provided that the German Government will give the same declaration?"[7]

Bell had some support for this appeal and it encouraged him to put down a resolution on the theme at the May Meeting of the Convocation of Canterbury. Archbishop Cosmo Lang, who did not approve of his letter to *The Times*, because he thought Germany would not keep any agreement they made, persuaded him not to put the resolution, but promised to remonstrate against the growing clamour for reprisals, in his presidential address. The agreement between the Archbishop and the Bishop was that Lang would speak against the growing demand for reprisals and Bell would simply present a motion expressing sympathy with the victims of German air raids on Britain and admiration for their courage. But Bell could not contain himself and, to the Archbishop's dismay, he went on to discuss the very question of night bombing which it was understood he was to avoid. Lang was very angry and rebuked him later. Many of his fellow Bishops also thought he was out of order. The line that Bell was taking brought him increasing unpopularity from church and state.

The Blockade

In both wars Britain attempted to intercept all trade going to Germany. This included, naturally, armaments but also food and daily necessities. Once Germany held the whole of continental Europe, with few exceptions, this meant the blockading of friend and foe alike. One of the most devastating effects of any action against Germany in the First World War had been the Allied blockade. Bell must often have heard Bonhoeffer, among others, tell of the terrible conditions under which the Germans lived as a result of this blockade. The privation caused was felt in the Second World War not only, or even principally, by Germany, but in the many occupied countries which were our Allies: Norway, the Netherlands, Denmark, Belgium, Greece, for example. After the war many stories were told of starvation in Holland. The food provided in the occupied countries was taken away to feed German troops, who were deprived of their usual imports.

On 27th January 1942, Lord Ponsonby, concerned about the effect this might have upon the attitude of our Allies towards Britain, asked for a government statement in the House of Lords. Bell spoke in his support. By now, Bell had learnt that the winning of the war was the sole concern of the government and he admitted this to be priority number one. We had long since passed the time of negotiation and we were in the midst of a life and death struggle. He had not given up hope of a resistance coup in Germany, but it looked less likely to be successful. As a patriotic Englishman he believed that eventually the Allies would win. He saw that when the tide turned, we should need the aid of these occupied countries whom we would call upon to help us liberate them from Nazi rule. It was, therefore, important that the people in those countries whose plight was certainly due to Germany's failure to live up to her responsibility, should not despair or be too weak to resist. He also appealed on humanitarian grounds. The reply from the government was unsatisfactory. They had sent some grain to Greece through the International Red Cross, but there was no real attempt to address the problem. All that could be said was that it was Germany's responsibility to feed these people, and that even if we sent food it would be taken away from them by the Germans. The blockade was justified in that it weakened Germany and was obviously effective. Bell could not accept this answer.

On 22nd April, he called together some twenty friends from different sections of the Christian Church and formed the Famine Relief Committee. Without government support, the Committee could take no action, but it could inform the Ministry of Economic Warfare about the effect of the blockade. This was done by periodic reports. Bell pressed his case again and again, making speeches, having private conversations with Lord Halifax and Anthony Eden as well as with the Minister of War (Lord Selborne). He never let up. He tried to avoid embarrassing the government. But sometimes he had to go public with speeches in the House of Lords and in Convocation, as well as in letters to *The Times*. He contrasted the minor irritations of our shortages with the desperate plight in Belgium and Greece. At one point the Committee was prepared to send dried milk and vitamins for children, nursing and expectant mothers, sufferers from deficiency diseases and so on. All the government had to do was provide 'navicerts' (navigational certificates testifying that the ships were not carrying military supplies) and allow them through the blockade. Something of Bell's frustration comes out in the final report of the Committee when the war in Europe was over and the feeding of Europe became a wider responsibility:

> "It would have been obvious to all intelligent people that our food blockade of the continent of Europe would bring untold torture and sufferings to our friends and allies and would do little or no harm to our enemy. . . History will judge our government harshly for its futile persistence in a policy of total blockade of foodstuffs".[8]

While Bell was engaged in this campaign, he kept up continuous correspondence with neutral countries, especially Sweden and Switzerland.

In Sweden he had many friends from his work for the Universal Council for Life and Work and in Geneva he had the Provisional Committee of the World Council of Churches and Visser 't Hooft. In addition Bonhoeffer was often in Switzerland and took every opportunity to keep in touch with his English Bishop.

Notes

1. G. K. A. Bell, *Christianity and World Order*, p. 92.
2. G. K. A. Bell, *The Church and Humanity*, Longmans, Green & Co., London, 1946, p. 32 – from a speech in the House of Lords, 13th December 1939.
3. *Op. cit.*, pp. 97–101.
4. *Ibid.*, p. 101.
5. *Chichester Diocesan Gazette*, January 1940.
6. *The Church and Humanity*, p. 56.
7. *The Times*, 17th April 1941.
8. *The Bell Papers* in Lambeth Palace Library, Vol. 59, part 2. (ff. 338–597), quoted by Jasper, *op. cit.*, p. 275.

7 The Conspiracy

The British government, as well as the German, tried with varying success to persuade the neutral government of Sweden to give support to their side in the war. Sweden was scrupulously neutral and resisted all blandishments, although there was little doubt that the people were largely on the side of the Allies. The invasion of Norway had shaken them and a considerable amount of underground help passed between the two countries. Germany handled Norway with greater care at first because of Sweden. Bishop Berggrav was clearly anti-Nazi and made no secret of his opposition to the invasion of his country. The case of Berggrav made it important that some church leader should go to Norway and the *Abwehr* chose Dietrich Bonhoeffer to accompany Count von Moltke. They succeeded in persuading the German occupying powers not to do anything rash with the rebel Bishop. Bonhoeffer did not meet Berggrav but he learned a great deal about the Church Resistance in Norway and the help being received from Sweden. For this reason, he was eager to get to Geneva to report to Visser 't Hooft. He was in Norway 10th–16th April 1942. On return to Germany he requested permission to make a journey to Switzerland. No questions were asked because it was assumed that the journey was all part of the attempt to keep the world churches favourable to Germany. Within three weeks of his return to Berlin Bonhoeffer was in Zürich, writing letters to his twin sister in Oxford and to Bishop Bell. He went to Geneva on 14th May. He was disappointed to find that Visser 't Hooft had left for London with a message from the controversial Adam von Trott. Visser 't Hooft saw Stafford Cripps, who passed the message to Anthony Eden. The resisters in Germany were anxious to have their efforts recognised in London. They could hold their military support only as long as London was prepared to treat fairly with an alternative, democratic government. If their resistance was to result simply in handing Germany over to be humiliated by their enemies, they could not carry the support of army officers who abhorred the very idea of treason. Their objective was to form a sovereign government which would negotiate honourable terms with a British government.

Although Bonhoeffer was disappointed that he missed Visser 't Hooft, while in Geneva he learned that Bishop Bell was to make a visit to Sweden 'for three weeks commencing 11th May' as a telegram to Visser 't Hooft indicated. Back again in Germany he therefore arranged for a visit to Sweden. Plans were afoot for a dramatic *coup d'etat* to which Bonhoeffer was privy. Its success would, of course, depend on having the right support in Germany. And that depended upon some word of encouragement from Britain. A message and an explanation had to be communicated to Churchill, or at least to Anthony Eden. The obvious channel was through Bishop Bell, who, as a member of the House of Lords, had immediate access to Anthony Eden. It is likely that the conspirators overestimated Bell's influence and underestimated his unpopularity. However, for a meeting with Bell, Bonhoeffer was the natural choice as courier.

Bell's Visit to Sweden

Earlier in the year, a rather limited air service between London and Stockholm had been started. The British government made use of it to reestablish cultural links between the two countries. T. S. Eliot went as one of the first visitors. Bell's long-standing contacts with Sweden meant that he was a good choice for a visitor to establish links with the Swedish Church.

Papers in the Public Records Office indicate that there was more in it than this. Churchill had in mind a possible union of Scandinavian countries with Britain and was anxious to hear from Bell about the relations between Sweden and the occupied countries of Norway and Denmark. Even more significant would be to obtain confirmation about the attitude of the churches in Finland to the Russian invasion. All this makes sense of Bell's diary, written day by day during his visit. The atmosphere of the wartime journey is caught from the first by this diary:

"May 13, 2.46 (Swedish time) arrived at Stockholm airport after a pleasant flight in a plane with a Norwegian pilot and two crew. No other passenger. Wore oxygen mask for an hour and a half (alt. 23,000 feet). Coffee and sandwiches towards the end of the journey. On arrival, owing to a misunderstanding, there was nobody to meet me. Fortunately there was a British Legation car at the airport and the air attaché, Mr. Fleet, met me in Stockholm and took me to the hotel, where I slept comfortably. At 9am next morning, the chaplain who should have met me, the Revd C. H. Jones, brought my programme and gave me some Swedish currency. Train at 11.30 to Upsala. Lunch with Archbishop Eidem. . ."[1]

For about two weeks he travelled around Sweden, meeting groups of church people from Sweden, Norway and Denmark. Always questions were asked about Finland. There were also pertinent questions about the German Resistance. Bell gathered considerable information about church and military personnel who were opposed to Hitler. He also probed the attitude of Swedish church leaders to what was happening in Finland. He met a German Foreign Office official at a Red Cross committee and asked about the possibility of Christian work in Estonia. The German was polite and courteous, but unyielding. Bell obtained information about Bishop Berggrav of Norway as well as the special and favourable treatment meted out in Denmark to the churches and other public institutions.

Then on 26th May came an event which later he described as 'my dramatic encounter with a German pastor'. In his diary, however, it sounds almost planned. After dinner with old friends – Archbishop Brilioth and the widow of Nathan Söderblom – he describes that meeting on the day it happened:

> "Ehrenstrom fetched me and took me to meet Schönfeld . . . Most interesting conversation. Gave me copies of sermons for English prisoners of war in Germany. Provided by Gerstenmeier of *Evangelische Hilfswark* [the main Protestant Relief Agency]. These sermons were by well-known ecumenical personalities, like Lilje. He told me of an office in Geneva which worked for prisoners of war and asked about official contacts. He told of many foreign office sympathisers who had protected YMCA youth etc. Then spoke of a very important movement inside Germany, first from the Protestants, but now linking up with Catholics. Eminent churchmen had spoken out about human rights".[2]

The diary goes on to say – in note form – that Schönfeld talked of resistance to National Socialism, a movement to remove Hitler, Himmler and the SS, with strong army support. This nearly happened in December 1941, when officers refused to go to the Russian front. Then no lead was given and the resistance went silent. More hopeful plans now, but the question was, 'Would England after such a coup, deal with the changed government?' Such a revolution would require the army, but they had no confidence that England would do better than at Versailles. The army would only support such a coup if they could be sure that England would deal honourably with a non-Nazi Germany. 'Would government in England support such revolution and could one hope for a negotiated peace if the gangsters were removed?'

Bell was suspicious of Schönfeld, because he represented the official German Church and he knew enough of the situation in Germany to realise that he was apparently dealing with the 'other side' from the Confessing Church. He did not know that Schönfeld was a very brave man who had come to Sweden via Geneva and had taken very great risks. He told Bell of the plans for a coup, which would mean the arrest of the Nazi leadership, who would be put on trial for crimes against humanity.

At this stage, there was no plan to assassinate Hitler. Bell asked for information in written form and Schönfeld provided it despite the obvious danger if it fell into the wrong hands. It contained the names of those who would support the coup. The document listed several groups working secretly for the overthrow of the Nazi government. During 1941 and 1942 these groups, according to Schönfeld, had come together and formed a powerful opposition, with a network throughout the whole of Europe. There were three main sections, now all working together:

(a) high-ranking officers and senior civil servants;
(b) former leaders of trades union and other workers' organisations, now banned;
(c) the churches, including Protestants led by Bishop Wurm and Catholics led by the Fulda Conference of Bishops.

The coup was well worked out. After the arrest of the Nazi leadership, a military government would be formed which could treat with Britain and later prepare for democratic elections. The document went further with detailed proposals for a Federation of European states and a special section on relations with the Soviet Union. It was a highly sophisticated plan and the list of people involved was impressive. The coup stood every chance of success – provided it could be encouraged by Britain. All of this depended upon Britain giving some kind of sign that they would not take advantage of the situation to invade and that, when it was completed, Britain would be prepared to discuss peace with a government purged of Hitler and Himmler. Bell knew that he would have to check that this was more than a pipe dream and so far he had only Schönfeld's word to go on. A few days later he had confirmation when he met his trusted friend Dietrich Bonhoeffer on Whitsunday, 31st May 1942. Bell was then in Sigtuna, an ecumenical and educational centre not far from Stockholm.

The meeting with Bonhoeffer was totally unexpected. Without Schönfeld's knowledge he had brought identical information and there was no longer any doubt in Bell's mind. Of Schönfeld, he had been suspicious, but he trusted Bonhoeffer completely. He had, of course, to make sure that the plan was viable and that Bonhoeffer was privy to all the information necessary. The discussion that followed was detailed. George Bell was a very good questioner and few things escaped him when he wanted to know the facts. Then Schönfeld joined them and they had a thorough discussion of the chances of success and the people who could be relied upon. Bonhoeffer was able to append a further list of conspirators to Schönfeld's document. After further discussion and questioning, Bell was satisfied that the conspiracy was genuine and had a reasonable chance of success.

But he knew that it was not going to be easy to convince the Foreign Secretary, Anthony Eden, in London. Unless he did, the plan was off. The military would not go ahead without some support from Britain. Bell also knew that, while the resistance movements in the occupied countries were given every support from London, the resistance in Germany was viewed with much suspicion. Bell would have to argue that, even if the plan failed, Britain had nothing to lose by agreeing to deal with the conspirators. And if they did succeed, the war could be over before Christmas. It was a gamble, he knew, but with high stakes. For Bell, it meant an end to war and the beginning of peace – a time for healing.

London Rejects

Bell met Anthony Eden and presented the plan with the credentials of the conspirators. He put forward his arguments, but they were not taken as seriously as he would have wished. Eden was unsympathetic to Bell and had in fact expressed doubts about the wisdom of sending him to Sweden at all. Bell could not squeeze a word of encouragement out of the war machine, which was apparently only interested in the total destruction of what Churchill called 'the monstrous tyranny'. By his logic, any suggestion that there was a 'good' Germany would weaken his appeal for an all-out effort. The enemy had to be totally black to justify the sacrifices, 'the blood, sweat and toil'. Also, in 1942, Bell's influence was weakened by the unpopular causes he had supported. The Vansittart policy held the field and that was interpreted in Germany as the annihilation of the German state. Churchill showed some interest at first, but on 17th July, Eden wrote to Bell, 'I am satisfied that it would not be in the national interest for any reply whatever to be sent'.

Bell pressed further, asking that at least some clear statement be made to allay the fears and suspicions in Germany that all Britain wanted was the annihilation of Germany. Could the Allies not say that they have no desire to enslave a Germany which has rid itself of Hitler and Himmler? That appeal had some effect upon Eden, but he was unable to go back on his earlier decision.

On 4th August, he wrote:

> "They [the conspirators] have so far given little evidence of their existence and until they show that they are willing to follow the example of the oppressed people of Europe running risks and taking active steps to oppose and overthrow the Nazi rule of terror I do not see how we can usefully expand on the statements which we have already made."[3]

Eden must have been fully aware of the totally different situation in Germany from that in the Netherlands or Norway or even France. The conspirators were in senior positions in army and state. Their whole strength lay in their secrecy. Once they were known they could be annihilated. In fact, after the July 20th 1944 attempt on the life of Hitler they were annihilated – thousands of them. They needed the encouragement which would enable them to win others to their cause. But no word came. In due course, Bonhoeffer and Schönfeld learned through their own channels that the British government was not prepared to take any steps or make any commitments which would encourage them. They were on their own. After this failure, the conspirators lost their strongest support.

Making the Distinction

It was a sad telegram that Bell sent to Visser 't Hooft in Geneva. 'Interest undoubted, but deeply regret no reply possible. Bell.'

Bell could not help the conspirators, but he could continue his fight to convince his country of the distinction between Nazis and Germans.

On 15th October 1942, he spoke to the Upper House of the Convocation of Canterbury.

> "I could wish that the British government would make it very much clearer than they have done that this is a war between rival philosophies of life, in which the United Nations welcome all the help they can receive from anti-Nazis everwhere – in Germany as well as outside – and would assure the anti-Nazis in Germany that they would treat a Germany which effectively repudiated Hitler and Hitlerism in a very different way from the Germany in which Hitler continued to rule."[4]

Bell's battle had not been entirely unsuccessful. He learned from German refugees that leaflet raids and a BBC broadcast to Germany, as early as July, had made clear that the British government understood the distinction between Germany and the Hitler government. That broadcast was much clearer than anything that Churchill or Eden had said in public in Britain. Bell tried to make the government declare its hand, and say to the British people what it was saying to the Germans. He had an unexpected ally. On 6th November, Stalin spoke in public declaring that a distinction must be made between the German people and the Nazi regime. As soon as he had obtained the text of what Stalin said and made quite sure of what he meant, Bell tabled a question in the House of Lords. He was persuaded not to persist – in the national interest! It was argued that the leaflets and the broadcasts were propaganda although of course true, but not suitable for publication in Britain where they might affect the war effort. Bell was not satisfied with this and in mid-December had a frank discussion with Eden. They agreed that he should not mention the leaflets or the broadcasts on the German Service of the BBC, but that he was free to ask a question on the policy of the government towards the Nazi state and what difference there was between that and dealing with Germany as such. The opportunity arose on 10th March 1943. It was already too late. Roosevelt and Churchill had met in January at Casablanca and affirmed that the war should be pursued relentlessly until *the unconditional surrender of Germany was secured.*

Bell had given up all hope of an encouraging word for the conspirators of 1942, but he still hoped to influence the attitude to Germany. It was no longer a matter of tabling a question but promoting a meaningful debate and this was possible when Lord Vansittart made a withering attack on Germany in the House of Lords, 11th February 1943. Bell spoke in response, accepting the fact of the atrocities and the need for action to prevent further atrocities. But he insisted that it was wrong to blame Germany as a whole. There were many in Germany who had protested, at the risk of torture, concentration camp and death:

> "To line up the Nazi assassins in the same row with the people of Germany whom they have outraged, is to make for more barbarism, possibly to postpone peace and to make quite certain of an incredible worsening of the conditions of all Europe when at last peace comes."

He then pressed his argument that a distinction must be clearly made, and did it without reference to the leaflets or propaganda broadcasts.

> "The remedy is to tell those inside Germany who are anti-Fascist that we want their help, that we will help them in getting rid of the common enemy, and that we intend that a Germany delivered from Hitlerism shall have fair play and a proper place in the family of Europe."[5]

Bell was able to return to the theme on 10th March when he put his question in the House of Lords. He argued that the strongest opposition to Hitler was the churches, Catholic and Protestant, and Hitler knew that the only hope of appeasing them was to persuade them that they were threatened with destruction just as much as the Nazis themselves at the hands of the Allies. Bell obtained from Lord Simon, the Lord Chancellor, as clear a statement as he could have hoped for:

> "I now say in plain terms, on behalf of His Majesty's Government that we agree with Premier Stalin, first that the Hitlerite state should be destroyed, and secondly that the whole German people is not (as Dr. Goebbels has been trying to persuade them) thereby doomed to destruction."

It was one of Bell's most successful debates in the House. It was also well reported, both in the press and the BBC German service. Friedrich Siegmund-Schultze, the veteran ecumenical leader of the German churches who had been exiled to Switzerland, heard the broadcast and sent a telegram from Zürich to Bell congratulating him.

We owe to Siegmund-Schultze the archival material on the growth of the ecumenical movement in Germany. His papers are deposited in Berlin, at the Evangelisches Archivzentral. Siegmund-Schultze was for years the editor of *Die Eiche* which during his editorship outlined the condition of those of Jewish origin in Hitler's Germany. It was after a careful survey which he intended to publish that he was deprived of his editorship and had to leave the country. From Zürich he followed events during the war and kept all the correspondence and press cuttings which were relevant to the development of the ecumenical movement and its attitude to the Church Struggle in Germany. In particular he kept copies of all his correspondence with the Bishop of Chichester and it is clear that he followed Bell's confrontation with his opponents. More than most, he recognised the importance of his victory in the House of Lords on this occasion. His telegram was appreciated by Bell who retained a great affection for the ecumenical leader. After the war they met and cooperated in the building of ecumenical relations between Britain and Germany.

There were others who appreciated Bell's achievement. Siegmund-Schultze's telegram assured Bell that opposition circles in Germany had reacted favourably to what they heard of his question in the House of Lords on 10th March 1943. Bell notified the Foreign Office of this news and received warm approval from Richard Crossman, at that time in the Political Intelligence Department:

> "The debate in our view was the best and most objective discussion yet held on the problem. For the fact that it was, we are largely indebted to you, for I think you set a tone which almost compelled a high and dignified level of discussion. Perhaps the greatest confirmation of this fact is that we have not found any reaction in German propaganda to the debate worth mentioning. The fact is it did not provide them with any ammunition." (25th March 1943)[6]

The Destruction of the German Cities

Those of us who went into Germany shortly after the end of the war were shocked at what we saw. Many have written about the horrors of Belsen and Buchenwald and I would not wish for a moment to under-play the stunning sense of demonic cruelty there. But we were also shocked by what we saw of the German cities and even small country towns. The saturation bombing of Hamburg, Cologne, Essen, Dresden was matched by the utter destruction of towns that had no conceivable military value. I remember driving by Jülicher and recalling the words of Micah and Jeremiah, "Jerusalem shall be ploughed as a field", or the words of Jesus, "Not one stone shall be left upon another". Then as one heard of the horrors of napalm bombing and civilians burnt alive, it was impossible to view it with a dry eye. Strong men wept!

This was the picture that Bell saw in his mind when he took up the most unpopular cause of being human in wartime. Our strength was growing and we felt able now to do to Germany what she had tried to do to us and more so. Military objectives became subordinate to revenge. It was the beginning of our terror bombing. Bell tried to enlist the influential William Temple in his cause. He knew that a question by the Archbishop in the House of Lords about the policy of bombing German cities with disregard of what we were doing to civilians would be better received than from him. Temple's reply was one of his least admirable utterances: "I am not at all disposed to be the mouthpiece of the concern which I know exists, because I do not share it". Bell was discouraged also from raising the question himself. He used other channels to make his views known and the expression of his concern at the indiscriminate bombing was well publicised.

On 20th September 1943, Battle of Britain Sunday, Bell was due to preach at the Commemorative Service in his Cathedral. He had admiration for the courage of those airmen who had defended Britain and to whom we owed so much, and would no doubt have spoken eloquently and without reserve in honour of those who had given their lives in the battle. But it was feared that he could not stop there. The Dean felt compelled to ask him to withdraw. Bell did not make an issue of it, but withdrew. He was feeling a new opposition – in his own diocese. But he persisted.

On 9th February 1944, he put his question in the House of Lords. As always he carefully discussed his arguments with those who could give him reliable information and he consulted with his fellow bishops, many of whom promised support, including the former Archbishop, Cosmo Lang, and Bishop Headlam. Although parliamentary business meant that the date was fixed months ahead, the timing proved unfortunate. The RAF had carried out a spectacular raid on Germany just before that date and it was greatly praised in the country for its daring.

Jasper, in his biography of George Bell, has preserved a reminiscence of Lord Woolton, who was an old friend. It refers to the day that Bell was about to speak in the House of Lords on this unpopular theme at an inappropriate moment:

> "I remember seeing him sit on the Bishops' Bench and I went to him and said, 'George, I believe you are going to make a speech'. He replied, 'Yes, I am'. I said, 'George, there isn't a soul in this House who doesn't wish you wouldn't make the speech you are going to make'. He looked a little downcast at that, and I said, 'You must know that. But I also want to tell you that there isn't a soul who doesn't know that the only reason why you make it, is because you believe it is your duty to make it as a Christian priest'. That was true: the House held him in the greatest respect, in complete disagreement."[7]

The speech caused a furore in the British press and the Services. It was badly received in the House of Lords and the cartoonists had a field day. Bell was depicted as naïve, 'a political bishop', pro-German, and with every possible misunderstanding of the cause he represented. Lord Vansittart was his fiercest opponent. But Bell was encouraged by the fact that of the massive correspondence he received, some of it violent, at least two-thirds of his correspondents approved of what he said. The Church Press was mostly favourable to him. The *Baptist Times* was outstanding in this, declaring that he 'deserves credit for raising in the House of Lords the question just now exercising many minds and causing some heart searching – as to whether the openly acknowledged policy of systematically obliterating cities – area by area – is a justifiable act of war'. In Sweden he had support for his courage. Captain Liddell Hart first quoted an RAF friend as saying 'a very large proportion of the silent public agree with the Bishop'.

Von Moltke

The Kreisau Circle in Germany was a spider's web of intrigue which held together many of the different opposition groups, and in its varied and uncoordinated way it was responsible for the major acts of resistance to Hitler. Its most important member, Count Helmuth von Moltke, had close links with England and Bell in particular. Lionel Curtis, one of the co-founders of both *The Round Table* and the Royal Institution of International Affairs (Chatham House), was a close friend of the family. Von Moltke was often in England in the 'thirties, entertained by Lionel Curtis, and British foreign policy was a frequent subject of discussion between the two men. Von Moltke and Lionel Curtis were thus mutually informed about each other's country in those grim days of Hitler's seizure of more and more power.

The Von Moltke Estate, at Kreisau, became the centre of the Kreisau Circle. Von Moltke himself made frequent visits to neutral countries, principally Sweden, from where he sent messages to his English friends. He was particularly anxious to let them know that the British propaganda was ineffective and wrongly conceived. He also informed the British government of the existence of the resistance in Germany. He invited his friend Lord Balfour to meet him in Sweden, but he could not obtain permission to go. Von Moltke's cousin, the German ambassador in Madrid, was also making overtures to the British government. The two approaches got mixed up at a high level. Von Moltke wrote a detailed message which he could not sign, giving full details of the resistance – he did not say 'conspiracy'. It was too dangerous to send this document in case it fell into the wrong hands, even in neutral Sweden. He therefore took his unsigned document to Sweden and gave it to one of his trusted contacts there – Johansson at Sigtuna, where Bell had met Bonhoeffer in the previous year. The idea was to arrange for its transmission to Lionel Curtis, but how? An American visitor who was to return from Sweden to the USA via England learned the contents by heart, and was told to communicate this to Bishop Bell, whom he already knew. This was done.

The letter which Bell then wrote to Lionel Curtis explained it all:

"A few days ago I had a visit from an American friend, just after his return from Stockholm. I saw him before he went to Stockholm on the YMCA prisoner of war business and again after his return. While there he was given a letter by a Swede called Johansson of Sigtuna, which was written to you by a German friend. It was five pages and unsigned, though the name, Johansson said begins with M, and he is known to be a prominent leader of the opposition and he had left the letter on his way back to Germany from Norway. [The Kreisau Circle had strong links with the Norwegian resistance, particularly Bishop Berggrav]. At the beginning of the letter he refers to Michael [Michael Balfour] and Julian [Julian Frisby], the implication being that they were friends of yours.

"The letter was very secret and it was realised that it was quite impossible to bring it over to England. I know Johansson and when I was in Stockholm myself last year I saw a lot of him and from time to time he sees German churchmen. My friend was asked to memorise as much as he could of the contents of the letter and these contents were passed on to us by word of mouth and subsequently written in a memorandum, a copy of which I enclose. In sending it he says, 'I fear that my notes were not adequately taken to give you a full content of the letter'. As he was only two or three days in London before flying back to the USA and did not know how he could get into touch with you personally he was asked by Johansson to give any information that he had obtained to William Paton and to me. William Paton had died and I was the only person who could be reached. The typed memorandum does not give one the full impression that conversation gives, but you will gather something from it. The particular desire which the German voiced was that a thoroughly trusted Britisher should if at all possible be placed in Stockholm in connection with the British Embassy, someone sensitive to the opposition with whom the opposition could establish contact. It would never do to have such an arrangement as part of the Secret Service: on both sides information is often got from the same sources and betrayal would be certain, in their view. In the letter, though not in the memorandum, the suggestion was made that if only somebody like Michael or Julian could be in Stockholm for this purpose it would make the whole difference. You, it was thought, would be sure to recognise who Michael and Julian were.

"There is a great inert mass in Germany now which, it was put to me, has gradually lost all confidence in a peace which would give Germany any chance. Those who are against Hitler are nevertheless thrown back upon their own people as they distrust Britain and distrust Russia for different reasons, and are terribly handicapped when thrown back to their own people because they do not know there what individuals they can trust. Still, in spite of Himmler, the soul of Germany, such men feel, is not lost."[8]

That letter, signed by George Chichester, was dated 14th September 1943.

The Failed Attempts to Assassinate Adolf Hitler

After the failure to obtain any encouragement from the Allies the conspirators in Germany did not give up. Hitler was leading his nation to disaster believing that he had divine protection. He proved right so many times when acting against the advice of his generals. The attack on Russia was sheer folly, but the German armies penetrated as far as Smolensk and their guns could be heard in Moscow. Hitler was nonetheless heading for defeat as the order to advance on Stalingrad soon showed. The conspirators saw that Germany needed a different government to talk to the Allies in defeat. If Germany could keep itself intact, in the end, they might force the Allies to treat with them. The need to eliminate Hitler became urgent. The various centres of resistance, now coordinated, hatched plots with daring and carried them out with courage. There were a few public protests against the Stalingrad venture, such as the White Rose pamphlet which brought the students of Munich out on to the streets. They were arrested, tried by a People's Court and executed.

It was in March 1943, that the conspirators thought they were nearest to success. A plot to assassinate Hitler on the Eastern Front and subsequent takeover by General Olbright, Chief of General Staff, seemed sure to succeed. The bomb failed to go off! Plot after plot staggered to unbelievable failure. Bonhoeffer was involved in all these plans. Then the cover of the *Abwehr* was blown when the Gestapo was allowed to investigate currency irregularities in Switzerland – perhaps associated with Bonhoeffer. Hans von Dohnanyi and Dietrich Bonhoeffer were arrested as well as many others in April 1943. It was a sorrow but no great surprise to Bell. This meant that Bonhoeffer was not involved in the ill-fated plot which all but succeeded in killing Hitler on 20th July 1944. A bomb in a briefcase was placed underneath the spot where Hitler stood. Someone moved the briefcase and when the bomb went off, Hitler was injured but not killed. His vengeance was fatal for Germany, and eventually Bonhoeffer and most of those whose names he had given to Bell in Sweden were among the executed.

Bell treasured his last message to him:

> "Tell him from me that this is the end but also the beginning – with him I believe in the principle of the Universal Christian brotherhood which rises above all national interests, and that our victory is certain. Tell him too that I have never forgotten his words at our last meeting."[9]

Bonhoeffer was executed on the 9th April 1945.

Bell continued his efforts to persuade the British government to abandon its policy of 'unconditional surrender'. In these efforts he was greatly helped by Gerhard Leibholz. The correspondence already quoted shows how close was the attitude of these two men in formulating a Christian approach to war and to the reconstruction of Europe after the war. It would require a separate volume to show the extent of their cooperation, but we are fortunate enough to have an essay in *Kirchliche Zeitgeschichte* by Ernst Albert Scharffenorth, called "The Task of the Church in Wartime: the Contribution of George Bell and Gerhard Leibholz to Great Britain's Policy towards Germany". The English summary of that essay will help to show its extent:

96

"The author shows how during World War II, Bishop Bell and the German refugee Gerhard Leibholz cooperated in the field of politics. Both men were convinced that Christians of belligerent nations had the common task of working for a just peace. It was, however, Leibholz who added a political dimension to that conviction. Without denying the responsibility of the Germans, particularly the German army, to free themselves of Hitler and the Nazi regime, Leibholz pointed to the fact that a policy based on the demand for 'unconditional surrender' must hinder such attempts. Bell followed this interpretation of the Allies' policy and worked secretly and publicly for a change in Britain's attitude".

The essay draws upon the correspondence between Bell and Leibholz and the publications of both during the war. Its range is limited to the period, August 1942–March 1943. [10]

After that, the arrest of Bonhoeffer and so many of his friends, the failure of the July plot and the subsequent massacre, all affected the Bishop deeply. He was irritated by Churchill's insensitive comment on the execution of so many brave men, that it was a case of 'the highest personalities in the German Reich murdering one another' (House of Commons, 2nd August 1944).

After the failure to assassinate Hitler

Bell pressed on more eagerly than ever now to save what could be saved from the wreckage. He asked to table a question in the House of Lords. He was persuaded that it was not in the national interest. He wrote to Eden on 27th July 1944, giving him information about the conditions in Germany. The intense control of civilians had turned Germany into a huge concentration camp and the church also was endangered. He suggested that it might be useful to open up communications with Sweden, exploring an escape route for those endangered and giving encouragement to those resisting. The Foreign Secretary gave him another negative reply. Bell seized every opportunity to put before the House of Lords the need to make known a constructive plan for Germany after the war. In this he was constantly opposed by Vansittart. Bell wanted a statement that Britain was determined to build Europe after the war on enlightened Christian principles, a new Europe in which Germany could play her part. On 19th December 1944, he reminded the House of the opposition of the German Church to Nazism and that the Churches should have a major role in the rebuilding of Germany on Christian foundations:

"I believe that in a time of distress and moral disintegration like the present, the Christian religion together with other spiritual traditions, Humanism, science, law, government, may still prove one of the great unifying forces of Europe, one of the principal agencies for assuring the fundamental rights and liberties of every European citizen."[11]

The Yalta Conference in February 1945 moved the frontiers and offered German territory to Poland in compensation for what Russia had taken from them. Later, at Potsdam in July–August after the German surrender, the division of Germany into four zones was determined. In consequence of these decisions a host of eleven million Germans evicted from the Eastern territories fled from the advancing Russian armies in terror, a million dying on the way. All this greatly disturbed Bell who maintained his cause to the end of the war and beyond, protesting and refusing to be silent. This adversely affected any hopes he might have had for preferment.

William Temple died in 1944 and Geoffrey Fisher became Archbishop of Canterbury. Bell would have welcomed a move to succeed Fisher at London, where as Bishop he could have exercised a greater influence than from Chichester. But it was not to be. No preferment for a man who speaks so plainly in wartime. Then at the end came the two atomic bombs on Japan and on 14th August 1945 he protested, saying that a just war was now no longer possible. He was not alone in face of the horror of what we had done to Japan. He recognised that with atomic warfare we had crossed a threshold. The war against Nazism was a just cause, although something more than war was needed to root out the evil. As Vaclav Havel said much later, 'Violence is not radical enough'. Like Havel he saw that Europe needed a spiritual revolution. The way in which we had conducted the war raised questions about Britain's fitness to lead that spiritual revolution.

Notes

1. *The Bell Papers* in Lambeth Palace Library, Handwritten Diary during visit to Sweden, 1942 – Vol. 279.
2. *Ibid.*
3. *True Patriotism*, edited Edwin Robertson, Collins, 1973, pp. 183–184.
4. Bell, *The Church and Humanity*, pp. 83–84.
5. *Ibid.*, pp. 86–94 (the full text of the speech).
6. *The Bell Papers* in Lambeth Palace Library, Vol. 38, ff. 271–292, *Cf.* Jasper, *op. cit.*, p. 275.
7. Jasper, *op. cit.*, p. 277.
8. Ger Van Roon, *German Resistance to Hitler*, New York (Van Nostrand Reinhold Company Limited), 1971, pp. 366–367.

9. Edwin Robertson, *The Shame and the Sacrifice*, Hodder & Stoughton, London, 1987, p. 276.
10. *Kirchliche Zeitgeschichte* (KZG), Part I, Göttingen & Berlin, 1988, pp. 94–115.
11. Bell, *The Church and Humanity*, p. 104.

8 Peace, Justice and the Unity of Europe

As the war was coming to an end, George Bell saw the need for three causes to be supported with all the strength he had. *Peace* had long been his special concern and he continued the battle for a *just* treatment of the German people. A third issue emerged which has a very modern ring still in the 'nineties. It was for the *unity* of Europe. The Western Allies had made a temporary union with each other and even with the Soviet Union, of which few of them really approved. The temporary nature of the union led to the formation of the United Nations Organisation, but with mistrust and lack of understanding. It was not long then before the Cold War led to two camps and two military organisations – the North Atlantic Treaty and the Warsaw Pact. And in the heart of Europe was Germany the enemy, to be re-educated and prepared for civilised society. Politically, there seemed little hope of a united Europe, despite Churchill's eloquent words. Bell saw these difficulties before the war ended and spoke of them to the House of Lords on 19th December 1944:

> "My Lords, there are many factors which make the realisation of European unity particularly difficult today. I agree . . . that a preliminary necessity is the ending of German military aggression. But, allowing for that, there are other obstacles. Some are material, arising directly out of the sufferings and losses of the war; some are political, and have to do with the decline of European Great Powers and the rise of World Powers with their desire for spheres of influence in Europe, but I think that the chief obstacle is spiritual, a profound distrust of nation for nation, Party for Party and citizen for citizen, together with an impending moral disintegration."[1]

That was a clear and shrewd analysis of the situation. The map had changed, the British Empire was intact, but the days of colonialism were over and all could see that independence would have to be granted to the British colonies. This was also true of the Dutch West Indies, Belgian Congo, the French Empire and the Portuguese Territories. Germany and Italy could not expect to regain the colonies that once they had, and Spain's dreams of empire were over. The days of great Imperial Powers were past. In their place came two Super-Powers: the Soviet Union and the United States of America. The war had impoverished Europe and only the generous American Marshall Aid had saved it, but even that only emphasised the emergence of a Super-Power. The two World Powers soon faced one another with hostility. Both wished to avoid a war and both felt the need to control part of Europe 'in self-protection'. The only hope for Europe's self-determination was unity. And as Bell rightly pointed out, the countries of Europe did not trust each other. Not only did an iron curtain fall over Europe but each country strove with more or less success to preserve its sovereignty.

Bell now saw that sooner or later there would have to be a European Community. This was against the tradition of Europe's nationalism. To acquire a secure lasting unity needed something more, and deeper than a political impulse. He appealed to the common culture of Europe based upon four 'spiritual' traditions: 'the Humanist tradition, the scientific tradition, the tradition of the law and government and the Christian religion'. From that list it is clear that he meant by the word 'spiritual' something much wider than 'religious'. Victor Frankl, founder of the Third Vienna School of Psychotherapy ('Logotherapy') defined 'spiritual' in a sense that Bell would have understood:

"Within the frame of logotherapy 'spiritual' does not have a religious connotation but refers to *the specifically human dimension.*"[2]

Bell, however, singled out the religious element as the most important of the four. The Humanist was largely responsible for the liberal and humanitarian elements in European civilisation; the scientific for the part played by individual collaboration in European culture; the tradition of law and government, while less unified, distinguished European from Asiatic societies.

He made a grander claim for the Christian religion:

"Which provided the original bond of unity between European peoples and has influenced every part of Europe and every section of European society."[3]

He pointed out that of all the crises in Europe at that time, the most serious was the spiritual crisis in the broadest sense of that word. Frustration and despair were leading to moral disintegration which was accentuated by material disintegration. European culture stood in danger of dissolution, unless a common purpose could be found for it. Unlike some, who saw Europe threatened by Communism, he felt the real enemy to be Nihilism, defined as 'the attitude of destruction and negation which calls evil good and good evil'. Once again he argued that the only consistent resistance throughout the war, in all countries but with varieties of intensity, had been from Catholic, Protestant and Orthodox Churches:

> "Men of all Churches have stood together against dictatorship, and have stood side by side with men of the resistance movements."

His friend, Dietrich Bonhoeffer must have been in his mind as he said that. For he knew that Bonhoeffer had allied himself in the *Abwehr* with those who had been in conspiracy to assassinate Hitler and take over the government of Germany. It had failed. Thousands had died. Bonhoeffer and those closest to him were in prison and with little hope of survival. The resistance had not been equal in all countries but always it had been there. He reminded the House of Lords of statements made throughout the war by leading churchmen, including the Pope. He expressed his opinion that Europe was ripe for a 'spiritual' renewal, despite the material and moral disintegration. He backed this up with his usual well documented evidence from Germany and occupied countries, in whose resistance he saw a real spiritual quality. And he concluded:

> "I believe that in a time of distress and moral disintegration like the present, the Christian tradition, together with the other spiritual traditions – Humanism, science, law and government – may still prove one of the great unifying forces of Europe, one of the principal agencies for ensuring his fundamental rights and liberties to every European citizen."[4]

In Defence of German Resistance to Hitler

Bell's speech in the House of Lords was made after the tragic attempt to assassinate Hitler on 20th July 1944. That had failed with disastrous consequences. What saddened Bell and others was that the attack was believed to be a last desperate attempt to save something of their future by a group of Nazi thugs. Bell spoke in defence of these brave men who had paid with their lives and in this he was joined by Gerhard Leibholz. The point that Gerhard Leibholz made most convincingly was that this was no last minute attempt by desperate men who knew that they had lost the war, but that the opposition had been in existence from the moment Hitler seized power. As his wife writes:

> "It requires really endless patience to explain to the English, again and again, the difference between the Nazi regime together with its adherents and the other Germany which had nothing in common with this."[5]

And as a Bonhoeffer herself, she knew. Bell spoke, Leibholz wrote and tried to publish. Both knew the truth of this continued resistance – and so, of course, did also the government. Leibholz eventually persuaded the *New English Weekly* to publish his article on the 20th July Plot. He argued against earlier interpretations, saying that the significance of the Plot had been played down and motives underlying it falsified. He maintained that what was in question was a movement grandly conceived and inspired by the same humanitarian motives as were held in the West. He also stated that the failure of the attempt on Hitler's life was a tragedy for the Allies too. The understanding of the explanation would determine the way Germany would be treated after the war. Bell had spoken much of this, but it was Leibholz who put the issue most clearly in a letter to the *Strand Magazine* after the end of the war in Europe:

> "Tens of thousands have gone through the fires of persecution, paying with their lives. For instance most of the leaders of the conspiracy of last July were upholders of the European tradition. And the stand of the Catholic and Protestant Confessional Churches had filled many people with a new religious vitality. I fear that the plans to put the German educational machinery under the permanent guardianship of the Allied Educational Board are bound to fail because they tend to degrade the trustworthy Germans into 'quislings' in the eyes of the German people. But without putting trust in these elements who are convinced that Germany must again become a European and Christian country Germany cannot be re-educated."[6]

Those of us who served in the Control Commission knew the wisdom of this advice although the general ethos of the occupation made it hard to follow. Leibholz urged the Allies to find the right people among the Germans, put them in the right places and then trust them. He felt that as soon as possible professionals should work under German control, limiting Allied control to the political field. His reason was clearly twofold: because there were competent Germans who could be trusted and of much higher quality than the Allies could supply, and 'to avert that national humiliation and despair which after the last war so greatly contributed to the present conflict'.

All this clearly expressed Bell's position also as the correspondence shows. But for Lord Vansittart it was a travesty of the facts. His criticism of the article was little short of insulting. A few weeks later, however, he had a much tougher article to deal with. This time by Bell in the *Contemporary Review* for October 1945. It strongly supported Liebholz's position with the factual material. The article was called "The Background of the Hitler Plot". Bell did not content himself with defending the attempt on Hitler's life as the act of trustworthy people, who had genuinely wished for a more liberal Germany. He knew that the charge that those who were making a last desperate effort to salvage something from a defeated Germany could not be contradicted by rational arguments alone. Incontrovertible facts were needed. He therefore went back to his meetings in Sweden in 1942, when Germany was not losing the war. He showed how this resistance had been courageously maintained by men of indisputable integrity. And he spoke, not of reports, but of his own meetings and his long experience and acquaintance with some of those involved. It is a masterly article and even persuaded Lord Vansittart to change his views.

Bell concluded with a statement about the price the conspirators had paid, including the execution of an estimated 20,000 men and women. The name of Bonhoeffer featured much in the article, 'one of the latest victims'.

His last paragraph is worth quoting:

> "They are all gone. But their witness remains. It is on the survivors of that opposition, in all parts of Germany, and on all others, both inside and outside the Church, who are inspired by liberal and humanitarian ideals and by a true love of their country, together with like-minded men in other countries, that the spiritual rebirth of Germany and the recovery of Europe depends."[7]

Christian Reconstruction in Europe

As early as 1943, an interdenominational body was formed in Britain to inform Christian opinion on international affairs and re-establish relations between churches which were severed by war. It was called the Christian International Service, chaired by Canon Charles Raven of Christ's College, Cambridge, a pacifist, and at that time on the BBC black list! The secretary was an old friend of Bell's, Dr. Franz Hildebrandt, one of his 'two boys', Bonhoeffer being the other. Naturally Hildebrandt turned to Bell for help. They discussed the constitution of the movement and Bell suggested that it be linked with the British Council of Churches. This proved a very important suggestion because at the world level the provisional structure of the World Council of Churches included a Department of Reconstruction and Inter-Church Aid. The British organisation was a national version of this and similar organisations were formed later in other countries. The Christian International Service developed after the war into Christian Aid with one very significant branch in the British Zone of Germany, called 'Christian Reconstruction in Europe'. It was set up in an Officers' Mess in Bünde in Westphalia with full approval of the Control Commission (British Zone). At the earlier stage when Raven was chairman, it had in mind simply information and the healing of broken relations.

The material reconstruction and the resettlement of displaced persons was so vast once the war was ended, that nothing short of an international enterprise of military proportions would do. This task fell to the United Nations Relief and Rehabilitation Administration (UNRRA).

'Christian Reconstruction in Europe' concentrated upon the rebuilding of Church life in Germany, in collaboration with the Religious Affairs Branch of the Control Commission. The British organisation gave encouragement in the renewal of church life and helped the churches to play their part in the restoration of national life. At first, this could only be by the provision of essentials like bicycles, but later led to visits to and from Germany. There were other National Committees in other countries, and Britain then saw the importance of involving George Bell. It would have been difficult to keep him out! The various national committees raised money for their work and Geneva acted as co-ordinator preventing too much overlap. The Church of England set up a small committee under Bell's leadership in November 1944 to study what help could be given. Bell was not slow and by February he had persuaded the Church of England to be responsible for raising £250,000 towards a national appeal for £1 million. He suggested this be shared among dioceses and committed Chichester to £10,000. In March he was in Paris learning of the needs of French Protestants. His correspondence with occupied countries was voluminous and he rejoiced in the display of Christian solidarity across Europe. Mark Boegner, the veteran President of the Protestant Federation of France, describes Bell's visit to Paris in his autobiography, *The Long Road to Unity*.

> "On the 10th March, the Bishop of Chichester arrived in Paris, delegated by the Archbishop of Canterbury (Geoffrey Fisher) to visit the Protestant Churches of France. We were overjoyed to welcome him in our home, more than four years after Mrs. Bell and he had welcomed us in theirs. He preached in Passy on the Sunday, 11th March, and on the same day in the Anglican Church in the Rue d'Aguesseau. Several meetings gave him an opportunity of talking with the Parisian pastors. It was a great essay in ecumenical education, made particularly fruitful by his infectious serenity and his great knowledge of the Churches. Already I could foreseee in him the man who would

one day inherit the responsibility of piloting the World Council of Churches through the reefs it would be bound to encounter."[8]

Although the committee was concerned with all Europe, Bell's special concern remained with Germany. The small Anglican committee grew into the larger National Committee and George Bell became the joint chairman with the General Secretary of the Baptist Union, the Revd. M. E. Aubrey, C.H.

Bell's Visit to Germany

As soon as hostilities ended in Europe, Bell was enquiring about the possibility of a visit to his friends in Germany, not a personal visit but to meet the church leaders who had stood firm against the Nazi inroads. He wanted to learn at first hand what the situation of the churches was – not only materially but spiritually. And they wanted to see him. In August he was listing the people he wanted to see: Bishop Wurm, Praeses Koch and Dr. Dibelius. He sent messages to them of course, but he wanted to meet them again face to face. Some of them had been his colleagues in the difficult days before the war in the Ecumenical Movement.

In his letter to the Chaplain General of the British Forces in Germany, he pointed out that the German leaders, including Bishop Wurm, had asked to see him and that Visser 't Hooft had briefed him about the difficulties in the German Evangelicial Churches. As he did not speak German he asked if he could take Gordon Rupp with him as interpreter. The Revd. Gordon Rupp was a Methodist minister with good German and an unrivalled knowledge of the intricacies of the German churches' situation.

There is also a very important letter about this time to J. H. Oldham which outlines the policy Bell thinks the government should take in relation to the churches in Germany.

1. The freedom of religion should be granted to the regional churches, with facilities to hold synods and communicate with each other, printing, publishing and the right to receive foreign visitors.
2. Bishop Wurm should be recognised as the head of the Confessing Church and be permitted to carry out his duties in ways deemed best to him.
3. The German Church leaders should receive encouragement and their independence of control from the occupying Powers be made clear.[9]

Bell also persuaded the Archbishop of Canterbury to write to the Secretary of State for War asking permission for representatives to visit German Church Leaders and for them to attend approved conferences outside Germany. All this took a long while to bring fully into effect, but it was not forgotten. Meanwhile, two names kept appearing in all correspondence: on the German side, Bishop Wurm; on the British side George Bell. Guy Clutton Brock, writing from Berlin, as Religious Affairs Officer, to Sir Wyndham Deedes on 19th August 1945, urges a visit by Bell:

> "If you ever see the Bishop of Chichester, make him push the powers that be to let him come out and see the Confessional folk in Berlin. They are longing to see him. I am pushing terribly hard from this end."

However, it was not until October 1945 that his visit took place. Meanwhile an historic meeting took place in Treysa at the end of August, when almost a hundred delegates from the German Evangelical Churches looked at what they had done during the Church Struggle. However, it is surprising to find little reference to it in Bell's correspondence or public speaking. He later saw the real importance of that conference, but for the time being his heart was full of the tragedy now facing the eleven million Germans from the Eastern Provinces trekking westward in the frightful conditions of post-war Germany.

Attlee had recently been elected Prime Minister in place of Churchill and, therefore, represented Britain at the Potsdam Conference of Allied Leaders, 17th July–2nd August 1945. It was to him that Bell turned in his deep concern for the fate of millions of Germans, mostly civilians and predominantly women, children and old men. A deputation of church leaders from the principal denominations in Britain, headed by Cyril Garbett, Archbishop of York, met the Prime Minister on 13th September 1945. Bell was in the delegation and as usual in possession of all the facts available. He did not hesitate to remind Attlee that, when he was presenting the decisions of the Potsdam Agreement to Parliament on 16th August, he had assured the House that provision would be made for the reception of the German refugees in the west. He had also said that if the problems became considerable, the expulsions would be held up until an enquiry had been made. These promises had not been honoured. The situation was desperate and neither an enquiry nor halting of the expulsions had occurred. Instead, the problem had become worse by the crowds of fugitives from Russia, Poland and Czechoslovakia, who had joined the trek westward. The delegation came away with nothing. And it is significant that the biographies of both Attlee and Garbett do not mention the meeting! Attlee, as well as Bevin, then Foreign Secretary, were aware that the Russians were having their way and that the Americans were not prepared to interfere or tolerate interference.

In fact, there was no adequate assessment of the refugee problem until 1948 at the joint conference of the World Council of Churches and the British Foreign Office in Hamburg Town Hall. Then, for the first time the extent of the problem of the three groups of refugees was revealed: German refugees from the lost provinces; *Volksdeutsche* – nationals of German origin in Czechoslovakia, Poland and Russia; and Displaced Persons (forced labour for Germany's war machine). At the meeting on 13th September nobody had the full facts, although Bell was the best informed. The Prime Minister listened and promised that everything that could be done would be done and welcomed their support. He thought that the task of the Churches should be primarily to educate public opinion. Bell took this to mean that the public should be made aware of the terrible things happening and try to influence governments. I am not sure that Attlee meant all this, but undoubtedly he was concerned. Churchill, also, in his famous 'iron curtain' speech expressed his deep concern.

On 19th October, Bell moved a resolution in the Upper House of Convocation (Canterbury) deploring the deportations and urging the Allied governments to do all they could to alleviate suffering. Similar resolutions were presented to both Houses of Convocation of York. It was becoming clear that you could not keep Bell away from Germany much longer. With the approval of Field Marshal Montgomery, at that time British Commander in Germany, the Bishop of Chichester visited Germany and saw his friends from 18th to 30th October 1945. His first appointment of importance was in Stuttgart on 19th October, where the German Evangelical Church leaders met the representatives of the World Council of Churches, and there the German Church leaders pronounced the now famous Stuttgart Declaration – the Confession of Guilt. But this conference had been preceded by the Treysa Conference, to which we must return before looking at the importance of Stuttgart.

Treysa and Stuttgart

On the evening of 27th August 1945, more than eighty representatives of the Evangelical Churches of Germany gathered in the Hessian town of Treysa to open the first national conference since the end of the war. It was opened with a service led by Schlatter whose texts were carefully chosen:

> "I will listen to what the Lord will say: he promises peace to his people, his saints – *but let them not return to folly.*" (Psalm 85 : 8)

That had been Bonhoeffer's text at Fanö in 1934 when the World Alliance threw its weight behind the Confessing Church. Schlatter added only the last phrase. The New Testament text was less topical if more necessary:

> "We will give our attention to prayer and the ministry of the word." (Acts 6 : 4)

The conference opened next morning with Bishop Wurm in the chair and with Niemöller and Schönfeld speaking. Almost every leader in the Confessing Church was there. It was a rallying of tremendous importance for the churches and research is still going on to determine from fragmentary reports and memories what exactly went on.

It ended on 31st August with meetings of the Council of Brethren of the Confessing Church, and then the first session of the Evangelical Church in Germany (EKD), which sought to bring together in one Federation all the regional churches, Lutheran, Reformed and United Churches. Bishop Wurm chaired the session, but the EKD was not officially established until 1948 when Otto Dibelius was elected its President. But already in Treysa, the German Evangelical Church found unity under Bishop Wurm and Martin Niemöller. They also found a voice of contrition, admitting their guilt for allowing so much wrong to happen in their country. They deplored their silence when they should have spoken. They regretted that their first concern was to preserve the Church. They had spoken too little against the treatment of the Jews. This was not a confession of guilt to the outside world but a recognition among themselves that they must take upon themselves the guilt of the nation. Niemöller was foremost in recognising the need for this. Already they began to write what later became the Stuttgart Declaration, to be circulated to representatives of the World Church in October. Bell was present at that later meeting in Stuttgart.

The October Visit

George Bell's interpreter Gordon Rupp described in his booklet *I Seek my Brethren* the significant events of that visit:

> "Appropriately, we left London from the Athenaeum in an army lorry. We had been delayed for twenty-four hours by fog, and this was to have curious results. We thus missed the first encounter on the 18th October between the members of the Ecumenical Delegation [mostly from Geneva] and the Council of the Evangelical Church in Germany. Our plane was a bucket-seated Dakota and as we sat facing the uniformed

soldiers, Bell took out pen and paper and wrote the speech of greeting he would make at Stuttgart. We landed at Frankfurt and drove south to the town of Tübingen [which was in the French zone of occupation) for a belated lunch. The French general asked Bell if he had any friends in Tübingen at which Bell blushed and said, 'Yes, one and you have him in prison' (it was Gerhard Kittel, the editor of the famous theological dictionary). We got to Stuttgart after dark and had some difficulty in finding the Staffelgasse where Bishop Wurm was living – finding the house marked by a white flag among the rubble. The two men had never met but were in fact old comrades greeting one another with evident warmth, and they had a long private talk together that night.

"Next morning, 19th October [1945], came the historic meeting. It took place in the upper room, an annex to the *Bibel Anstalt* [this was the *Privilegierte Bibelanstalt* which produced most of the academic publications for the Bible Societies] the members of the Council sitting intermingled with their ecumenical visitors at a long table, with two knots of chairs for those who could not get to the table. The proceedings were informal and the practical situation dominated – the most impressive part for me was the terrible picture Bishop Dibelius gave of the Church in the east, and of the pastoral needs.

"Then, if I remember correctly, Hans Asmussen (who said that morning that in prison he had read all Shakespeare seven times – 'without some things one can live; without Shakespeare one cannot live') handed round copies of a typed statement, which had been written and was indeed dated on the previous day. Bishop Wurm dictated two or three minor alterations, for the sake of clarification and of style."[10]

After a long discussion it became the text of the Stuttgart Declaration by the Protestant Churches of their acceptance of guilt.

The Stuttgart Declaration

It was on the basis of this confession of guilt that the representatives of the ecumenical movement met under God with the German churches, seeking forgiveness and trusting in the spirit of God to lead them into the future. The Declaration is so important that I quote it in full:

"The Council of the Evangelical Church in Germany at its session in Stuttgart on 18th October 1945 greets the representatives of the World Council of Churches.

"We are more thankful for this visit because we know ourselves to be united together with our people, not only in a solidarity (*Gemeinshaft*) of suffering, but also in a solidarity of guilt. With great pain do we say: through us endless suffering has been brought upon many peoples and lands. What we have often witnessed to in our congregations, we speak now in the name of the whole Church. We have indeed through long years fought in the name of Jesus Christ against the spirit which found its fearful expression in the Nazi tyranny (*Gewaltregiment*); but we accuse ourselves that we did not confess more boldly, did not pray more truly, did not believe more joyfully and have not loved more ardently. Now, in faith, a new beginning must be made in our churches. Grounded in Holy Scripture, with all earnestness looking to the only Lord of the Church, we go about to cleanse the Church from strange influences and to set our house in order. We hope that the God of grace and mercy may use our Churches as His instrument and will give them authority to preach His Word, and to create obedience to His will among ourselves and in our whole nation (*Volk*).

"It fills us with deep joy that in this new beginning we may know ourselves to be bound in solidarity with the ecumenical movement.

"We hope to God that through this common service of the Churches, the spirit of violence and of revenge which is once again active in our midst, may be abated in the whole world and the spirit of peace and love may come to triumph, in which alone tormented mankind can find healing.

"So we pray to God in an hour when the whole world needs a new beginning: *Veni Creator Spiritus*.

Stuttgart 18th October 1945"[11]

There was no specific reference to the Jews and that is regrettable, but the statement however general was clear: 'We know ourselves to be joined together with our people, not only in a solidarity of suffering, but also in a solidarity of guilt'. The ecumenical delegation understood it. Bell understood it too and in his greetings he filled in some of the details – with concrete reference to the persecution and attempted annihilation of the Jews, the deportation of Russians, Poles and Czechs. But his greeting was not to rebuke the omission of these things from the Declaration. He had after all drafted his statement in the plane flying over! He was happy to be with them, as a leader of the ecumenical delegation, as a Bishop of the Church of England, with greetings from many German friends in

England, as a brother in Christ and an old friend of the Confessing Church. He ended with a definition of the prime duty of the Ecumenical Movement and its relevance to the issues of the day:

> "to secure that the Church declares and maintains its vital interest as the body of the Incarnate Lord in the community itself, in public as in private conduct, in the social, national and international affairs of men."[12]

Further Travels in Germany

Over the next few days, Bell travelled in Germany, meeting old friends and others whom he had not known, but admired. Praeses Koch of West phalia, a great warrior in the Confessing Church; Von Bodelschwingh, the director of the Epileptic Colony of 'Bethel' near Bielefeld, which is also in Westphalia; the Catholic Bishop of Munster, Cardinal Graf von Galen, who resisted Hitler's excesses and even defied the Roman hierarchy when they were weak. All these were within easy range of the British Zonal Headquarters, scattered through a group of small towns. The Religious Affairs Branch was in Bünde/Westphalia. He had so far visited three zones of Allied occupation: Tübingen, in the French Zone; Stuttgart in the American Zone; and now in Westphalia he was in the British Zone. There was yet a fourth and that he entered when he travelled to Berlin, in the very heart of the Soviet Zone, but under quadripartite control with four separate sectors.

In Berlin, he began in the western part and his first and most urgent meeting was with the Bonhoeffer family. It was from his broadcast that they had learnt of Dietrich's death. They honoured him for the part he had played over many years and for his deep friendship with Dietrich. It was a sad group that he met, the remnants of a noble family, who had never wavered in their resistance to Hitler. They had suffered much. It was an emotional moment. They rose to meet him and Dietrich's mother handed to him her son's last present, his parting gift from Flossenberg: Thomas á Kempis' *The Imitation of Christ*. Bell leant to kiss her forehead. That kiss said much of shared sorrow and shared pride.

While in West Berlin, he visited the railway station at Lehrter and was saddened by the misery he saw. Gordon Rupp describes the visit briefly as he saw Bell moving among the suffering people:

> "There was the grim visit to the great railway station, the Lehrter Bahnhof, with platform and lines covered with thousands of human beings, mostly very old and very young, and teenaged girls with bleeding bandaged feet . . . And I remember Bell going slightly ahead of us, not able to speak German to them,

but stopping and smiling and patting children, and turning again and again to ask for facts and information – nothing to give but that obstinate compassion which persisted until the tiny streams of 'Christian Reconstruction' became the river we now know as 'Christian Aid'."[13]

There was no Berlin Wall at that time, although there were definite Sectors. Bell crossed over to the Soviet Sector to worship in the ruins of the great Berlin Church, the *Marienkirche*, where the Dean of the Church, Probst Grüber, maintained his heroic ministry. There Bell preached and again it is Gordon Rupp who gives us the eye-witness account:

"And then the unforgettable Ecumenical service in Grüber's *Marienkirche*, patrolled outside by armed Russian soldiers, part open to the sky. Within, a vast overflowing congregation of pale, bitter people stared at the high altar where stood four Christians in the uniforms of the occupying powers, Russian, French, American, British [Gordon Rupp was not aware that the Russian, perhaps the pleasantest of the four, was a convinced atheist!], and George Bell in the pulpit simply recalling the story of the man in the Gospels who was desperately sick, but whose four friends took him and laid him at the feet of Jesus".[14]

I am not sure whether George Bell was the first, but he was certainly not the last to compare those four friends to the four occupying powers. I must have heard more than a score of sermons in occupied Germany on that Gospel story! It took a long time to convince the Germans that the occupying powers were their friends, but it did not take long for them to realise the genuine compassion of George Bell, who was a friend of Germany. Probst Grüber also spoke at that Ecumenical service and startled the congregation with his abrupt question, "And are we yet alive?" Standing in the ruins of his own church, this man who had saved hundreds of Jews from the concentration camps, said that the fate of Germany hung on the connection between two sentences in the Lord's Prayer: 'Give us this day our daily bread' and 'Forgive us our trespasses as we forgive'.

The Unity of Europe

Bell returned to Chichester and, of course, he was not silent. Those scenes in Lehrter Bahnhof in Berlin were imprinted on his mind and he knew that they could be repeated thousands of times all over Germany. The awful sight of the 'Potsdam' refugees remained his deep concern. He took to heart Grüber's words. He worked for aid to the hungry of Germany and sought to show that while he did not underestimate the guilt of Germany, we were all guilty and in need of forgiveness. He became more and more convinced that 'there are few things on which it is more important to insist than the essential unity of Europe'. He had an opportunity to express this concern at a Christmas broadcast to Germany from the BBC, 23rd December 1945. It was the last in a series of Advent talks on 'Our European Heritage'. An earlier talk in the series was given by Gerhard Leibholz on Natural Law as a necessary foundation upon which Europe could be reconstructed. Bell paid tribute to this brilliant talk and took as his theme what Christianity means in the context of Europe as a whole.

He insisted that the great task for all thoughtful people in Europe, whatever their race, nation or political persuasion, was the making of unity in Europe. For this we had to go beyond politics to culture. There we shall learn the secret of our oneness. This was a bold step, because Hitler had indoctrinated a whole generation with the idea of German 'culture'. Bell talked of a European culture derived from Greece (the humanist), from Rome (the legal), and from the Renaissance (the scientific). They must be held together or they fly into fragments, and he added:

> "The tradition which has served supremely to bind the different elements and different peoples together is that of the Christian religion".[15]

He admitted the varying and often warring conditions within the Church and pleaded for a revival of the 'common Christian faith'. After an historical diversion he concluded that the principal goal 'should be the recovery of Christendom'. He does not look back to any ideal period in the history of Europe, but rather forward to a Europe in which justice is recognised, and not only justice, but love; not only law, but forgiveness. That stimulated his memory of Grüber in the *Marienkirche* of Berlin and he referred to his visit and the awful scenes:

> "This terrible war had indeed brought destruction untold. I was in Germany at the end of October, and I know something at least of what it means. I know too how the very spectacle of such colossal ruins numbs the spirit. I know with what a deep sense of frustration you are wondering when will it be possible, and how will it be possible, to begin to rebuild the destroyed towns? But important as this material building is, the springs of recovery rise in the spiritual zone, and believers and seers have a greater offering to make than engineers and technicians. For

the crucial need today is for the liberation of the soul of Europe, and this can only be done by a spiritual power from outside, by something which military force can never supply, nor our modern mechanised civilisation provide from its own resources".[16]

He admitted that we are a long way away from the liberation of the soul of Europe. The fires of war still smoulder and hatred is abroad among the nations. Ideologies still clash. There is much to be done. He ended his talk with the two truths which he believed were essential for a spiritual renewal and a common Europe: first the weak and hungry must be helped to survive, the strong nations must help the weak. The other truth is this:

"We all have to recognise that we have fallen short of the right standards of conduct to other people, and we have all to repent. No nation, no Church, no individual is guiltless. And as we would be forgiven ourselves, we must all be forgiving. Without repentance and without forgiveness, there can be no regeneration".[17]

Bell wrote the script with care and it was translated and read, possibly by Pastor Hildebrandt, who had read the wartime Christmas broadcast for him in 1942.

Over the next three months, Bell watched the progress of the Occupation and in particular the De-Nazification process and the War Crime Trials with growing concern.

Notes

1. The full text is in *The Church and Humanity*, pp. 158–164.
2. Viktor E. Frankl, *The Doctor and the Soul*, Penguin Books, 1979, p. 10.
3. *The Church and Humanity*, p. 179 (BBC broadcast, 23rd December 1945).
4. *Ibid.*, p. 164 (House of Lords, 19th December 1944).
5. Sabine Bonhoeffer-Leibholz, *The Bonhoeffers: Portrait of a Family*, p. 153.
6. Letter to the *Strand Magazine*, July 1945.
7. *The Church and Humanity*, p. 176.
8. Marc Boegner, *The Long Road to Unity*, Collins, 1970, p. 203.
9. *The Bell Papers*, Lambeth Palace Library, Vol. 43.
10. Gordon Rupp, *I Seek my Brethren*, Epworth Press, 1975, pp. 24–25.
11. *Ibid.*, p. 25.
12. *Ibid.*, p. 27.
13. *Ibid.*, p. 28.
14. *Ibid.*, p. 28.
15. *The Church and Humanity*, p. 178.
16. *Ibid.*, pp. 179–180.
17. *Ibid.*, p. 182.

9 The British Occupation in Germany

The victorious Allied Armies swept across Europe from the East and from the West, from the North and from the South. They 'liberated' the countries that had been occupied by Germany and 'occupied' Germany itself. Each cared for that part of Germany which they had fought over and then the whole question of occupation was tidied up at Potsdam at the end of July 1945. There had been three great powers – America, Russia and Britain. Then France became a great power overnight and four zones of occupation were allocated. Bell was most involved with what went on in the British Zone of Occupation. Each occupying power set up an administration which more or less coincided with the former German government. This was aided by the German system of independent provinces dealing with their own affairs, and a centralised 'federal' government to deal with foreign affairs and defence, as well as national finance. At first, the army administered and then within a year there was a civilian administration, known as the 'Control Commission of Germany' (CCG). Education and Religious Affairs came under one administration, headed by Colonel R. L. Sedgwick, whose religious affairs officer was the Revd. Arthur Cotter. Later a separate Religious Affairs Branch was set up, but religion and education always remained closely related in the British Zone of Occupation. Inevitably it was with these branches that Bell was most concerned.

De-Nazification

It was one thing to defeat Hitler's armies in the field, it was quite another to eradicate his 'philosophy' from the various aspects of life in society – schools, universities, churches, youth movements and so on. The occupying forces were all-powerful and could dismiss or imprison whom they chose. School teachers were dismissed because of their Nazi affiliation until there were not enough teachers left to teach the children. Textbooks were read for Nazi doctrine and banned, until there was an acute shortage of books in schools and universities. The churches were different. No one wanted to be accused of controlling the churches. It was therefore decided that the Church should purify itself from the cancer of Hitlerism. They knew who had collaborated and they could surely get rid of their Nazi leaders. The trouble was that the majority of the Church had gone along with the Nazi regime, at least in wartime, if only for patriotic reasons.

George Bell expressed the difficulty in an article he wrote for *Picture Post* on 8th December, 1945, in which he described the different factions in the German Church: some resisted bravely choosing Christianity rather than patriotism in the Hitler time; others threw in their lot with Hitler; whilst 'a moderate section' consisted in the main of those who wanted safety.

There were, of course, a large number who saw advantages in National Socialism, even if they disliked its excesses. Many of these thought at first that these excesses would destroy it, and later quietly withdrew their active support. A few joined the first group of those who resisted bravely. Many took the line that all questions of politics must be left to the State. Bell's major concern was with the Evangelical Churches in Germany. That is not to say that the Catholic Church was not compromised – it was. Klaus Scholder gives the example of Cardinal Bertram of Breslau, the senior German prelate, who on hearing of the death of Adolf Hitler, his Führer, drafted an order for a requiem mass to be said throughout the churches. Scholder's extensive study of the Churches in the Third Reich concludes that "under the Hitler regime any resistance from both Protestant and Catholic Churches came largely from individuals; officially the churches were interested above all in maintaining their *status quo*".[1]

For the Catholic Church, however, the occupying forces had a reference point outside Germany in the Vatican. There were those who thought that the Pope should be de-Nazified, but that was beyond the jurisdiction of the Control Commission!

The problem which could not be tackled systematically, because of its complexity, was that of the Evangelical Churches and clearly Bell was invaluable for unravelling that. He understood the nature of the Church Struggle and had long experience of the various territorial churches in Germany. They were of three kinds:

(a) *The Churches of the Prussian Union* which included the Prussian Churches united in 1817, with their provincial adherents in Westphalia and the Rhineland. Within these churches, there were 'German Christians', who had Hitler's support as the 'official' churches in their territories; and the Confessing Church, based upon the Barmen Declaration of 1934 and organised according to the Synod in Bad Oeynhausen in the same year.

(b) *The Reformed Churches*, which consisted of Calvinistic enclaves in Lippe, East Friesland and parts of Westphalia. These supported the Confessing Church, and were its strongest element despite smaller numbers.

(c) *The Lutheran Churches* which remained intact, refusing to divide into 'German Christians' and Confessing Church. They fought to maintain their independence and in so doing were often in danger of compromise. In Bavaria the Lutheran Church offered stiff resistance to the Nazis, particularly under the leadership of Bishop Meiser. This was not true of the other strong Lutheran Church, that of Hannover. While many of the people and clergy protested and suffered, among them Hanns Lilje, their Bishop Marahrens was suspected of compromise.

With the first two types it was possible for the churches to purify themselves early – this became clear at the Treysa Conference immediately after the end of the war – but the Lutheran Churches were more difficult.

The Case of Bishop Marahrens

It will illustrate both the difficulties which the Control Commission faced and the involvement of Bishop Bell, if we follow the case of Bishop Marahrens in detail. It is well documented in a study by Gerhard Besier entitled "*Selbstreinigung*" (Self Cleansing), devoted to the actions of the British Control Commission and Bishop Marahrens.[2] It shows that many of the Confessing Church were disturbed that Marahrens continued in office, because of what he had done and said during the Hitler period. He was both Bishop of Hannover and also Abbot of the Abbey in Loccum. As a Bishop he should have resigned, but the appointment of Abbot was for life. He did not resign as Bishop and no one felt able to remove him. The first report from Major Beattie, the Military Governor of Hannover, about him came in August 1945. The 'confidential' report is favourable to Marahrens, it points out that he has behaved very correctly towards the military government, cooperated in every way and made helpful suggestions about candidates for public appointment. After some evidence that Marahrens had been forced to compromise occasionally under the Nazis, he adds:

"I consider that Marahrens is a patriotic German and as such supported the German war effort (like many Lutherans he found the Treaty of Versailles a very heavy burden). But he was not a Nazi and certainly was never favoured by them".

Beattie pointed to the popularity of Marahrens, whose faults he says are those of the German character. "We may regret the German character, but we cannot alter it".

He concludes that it would be a mistake to dismiss the Bishop, but better to let the churches deal with him. Progressive elements in his own church may force him to resign. But that is not the job of the Military Government. This attitude was fairly typical among the officers of the military occupation. Marahrens defended himself against the accusations of his fellow bishops and did not take early retirement.

Marahrens attended the Treysa Conference, although he was not encouraged to come and there were some difficult moments there; but the worst occurred when he returned home on 28th August, to find that his papers had been raided by military personnel and some papers taken away. Major Beattie apologised when the Bishop protested and pointed out that the raiders were NCOs and not officers, who would have known how to behave! These NCOs had simply been over-zealous.

The issue was serious enough to attract Bell's attention and he was consulted. He wrote to Julius Rieger, who had just moved into Bonhoeffer's old house and pastorate at Forest Hill. Rieger replied that up to 1935, Marahrens had cooperated with the Confessing Church, fought against Ludwig Müller (Hitler's National Bishop) and took part in the Barmen Synod in 1934. He was never in the vanguard, but rather a 'retarding' factor. Niemöller, with his exaggerated style called him a criminal!

From 1935, Rieger said, Marahrens started cooperating with the 'German Christians' and supported Minister Kerrl. Rieger gave Bell eight relevant points which he used in subsequent efforts to help the Religious Affairs Branch make the right decisions about the Bishop and to encourage his friends in the German churches to act. The substance of these eight points is that Marahrens cooperated to preserve peace in his church (at any price), he was opposed to Niemöller and did not join in the protest at his illegal arrest and imprisonment, he had no intercessions for the victims of Nazi discrimination, he was weak on the Jewish question, over-supportive of Hitler, uncritical in his support of the war effort and took his actions with the authority, not only of a bishop, but as he constantly signed his letters, "the longest serving Bishop".

Rieger adds, "Marahrens will be able to make his point clear and persuasive, all the more as he has a personal charm which is difficult to resist. But it seems to me absolutley clear: there will be permanent trouble within the German Church, should this 'longest serving bishop' not make room for somebody else".[3]

The matter dragged on. Karl Barth in Switzerland lost patience with the British authorities. When in August 1947 Iain Wilson of the Religious Affairs Branch (by now separate from Education) met him in Switzerland, Barth insisted that the British should not have allowed Marahrens to retire gracefully but should have 'thrown him out'. John Gwynne, who was Iain's superior wrote firmly to Karl Barth that Marahrens had been allowed to continue in office a whole year before the Religious Affairs Branch had been formed and that they were late comers. But, in any case he would not take upon himself the authority to throw out a bishop of another church. Then he ended his letter with a paragraph that was bound to make Barth see red!

> "I would ask one final question. You told me you disapproved very strongly of the Bishop of Chichester having striven for a compromised peace before Germany had been completely beaten. Do you suggest, supposing I had the necessary power in England, that I ought to have him thrown out?"

Barth replied in typical fashion:

> "I would never dream of mentioning Bishop Marahrens in the same breath as the Bishop of Chichester (for whom here in Basel I have sought and obtained an honorary doctorate). I think that in the winter of 1939/1940, in his speech to the Upper House, which I have read in English, he was politically wrong, but that can happen to the best of men and never, never would I have thought that in any way that disqualifies him from church office. That I did not agree with him had never prevented me from regarding this man with the greatest honour".[4]

Barth's attitude to Bell and his high regard for him was shared widely among the church leaders in Germany. It was therefore inevitable that sooner or later Bell would have to be involved in the impossible tangle of the resignation of Marahrens.

The Involvement of the Bishop of Chichester in the Marahrens Affair

It is clear from the enquiry about Marahrens to Julius Rieger that Bell was concerned as early as September 1945.

On 5th February 1946, Hanns Lilje wrote to the Bishop of Chichester, asking if he would stop off on his way to London to talk with Marahrens. Lilje was hopeful that the matter might soon be settled with him. But he adds:

> "It is my impression that a short, private and completely confidential conversation between yourself and my bishop would do a lot of good. In view of your former relationship with my bishop, I venture to submit this idea to your consideration".

Bell was anxious that this visit should not be seen as an auxiliary of the Control Commission come to persuade Bishop Marahrens to resign. Colonel Sedgwick had some doubt about the visit, which he admitted might have to be a last resort. He appreciated Bell and said frankly that

"He knows more about the position than anybody except ourselves". Both Wurm and Lilje approved the private visit, but Sedgwick feared that it might be seen as the Church of England interfering with German Church affairs. Sedgwick wanted to have another try with Bishop Wurm. Again it failed. Colonel Sedgwick was driven to his 'last resort'. The private meeting was arranged at Kloster Loccum. Bell reported to Sir Gordon Macready the Regional Commissioner, on 17th June 1946. He described in great detail the progress of their conversation. After arrival, the conversation began at once and lasted for an hour. Marahrens confessed that he had been upset by one of Bell's articles (in *Picture Post*) saying that he was compromised. He protested that he and his church could not agree that he had compromised himself with the Nazis. He defended his Lutheran position, which meant telling of several private protests to Himmler.

"But after 1935", he said, "the Church Struggle became a sectarian dispute between the Council of Brethren (the Confessing Church) and the official Landeskirchen (territorial churches)". Marahrens, therefore, did not go public because he had no desire to be involved in this sectarian quarrel.

Bell allowed Marahrens to have his say. They visited the Abbey, worshipped together and continued their conversation. It was friendly and Bell said he made his points firmly but politely. It is useful to quote Bell's own account of the description he gave Marahrens of what the other churches saw as his compromising:

> "The points I made were that what the foreign churches complained of in him was his weakness, and his silence; that he had, especially in 1939, said some things terrible for a churchman to say in favour of the Führer. I told him that Foreign Churches regarded him as having an extremely responsible position just because of his seniority as a Lutheran Bishop; that he had been appointed a member of the Provisional Committee of the World Council of Churches in 1937, but that now the members of that Committee would not have him as one of their number. I also said that the younger German pastors and students placed all their hope in the World Council of Churches, and that fact must affect his own position in Germany. I said further, that if the Lutheran World Convention had asked him to resign, that showed that his interpretation of what Lutheran doctrine required in a Church leader *vis-à-vis* Hitler was unsound. I also said that if all the churches had behaved as he had done *i.e.* in silence and

weakness (I mentioned particularly his silence with regard to the Jews, his failure to protect Christians of Jewish origin in his own church, and his failure to safeguard freedom to preach the word of God) there would have been no church resistance in Germany".[5]

The effect of that visit was considerable and, although there were many delays and hesitations, Marahrens resigned at the 14th General Synod of the Hannover Church. The resignation was officially declared on 17th November 1947. The graceful retirement two and a half years after the end of hostilities was what Barth had objected to. The slow and civilised process was the only way and the Bishop of Chichester had played a major part in that.

That was not the end of Bell's interest in the Religious Affairs Branch, it was only the beginning.

The Religious Affairs Branch

On the 4th June 1946, the Military Governor of the British Zone of Germany, General Sir Brian Robertson, consulted with Bell about the establishment of an independent Religious Affairs Branch. There had been some agitation for this from the Education Branch, where it was decided that because of the complexity of church affairs in Germany, its section devoted to Religious Affairs considered the task no longer practicable. A memo to the Foreign Office (German Section) in London from the Education Branch reads:

> "German church affairs are now presenting problems of some magnitude and their wide significance makes it essential that there should be an adequate and responsible branch staffed by expert officers to deal with them. The need for such an organisation has been stressed by the heads of the major denominations in the United Kingdom and the Deputy Military Governor has already written to the Permanent Secretary on this subject. It is therefore requested that approval be given to the formation of a new Branch within the Internal Affairs and Communication Division to be known as the German Church Affairs Branch".[6]

The name was later changed to Religious Affairs Branch to prevent misunderstanding. This request was partly the result of continuing correspondence between the Bishop of Chichester and Colonel Sedgwick. Bell found an ally in the General Secretary of the Baptist Union, the Revd. M. E. Aubrey, who kept a constant eye on the treatment of the churches in Germany. Bell, however, was the leading spirit. He saw that without a fully recognised Branch staffed by people who knew what they were doing, the churches would never receive the help they needed to rebuild and renew after the devastation of war. He also helped Sedgwick to draw up a schedule of work for this new Branch.

Bell played a part in determining the structure of the Branch, arguing for adequate and high ranking staff. He supplied lists of suggestions, as did M. E. Aubrey. Sir Brian Robertson agreed to Bell's proposal that there should be a staff of 14 officers and nine other ranks. This was agreed in June 1946. Sedgwick proposed John Gwynne and Iain Wilson – the former as Controller and the latter as Head of the Evangelical Section. After the visit of delegates from the British churches in October 1946, Bell discussed the raising of the status of the Religious Affairs Branch. He argued at the highest levels that the Religious Affairs Branch was "not able to exercise sufficient influence when policy on a high level is being framed; and the Branch has not sufficient authority for obtaining for the churches the things they most need". He further added that it was important that the Branch should be able to deal directly with the Military Governor or his Deputy. As by now there were representatives of the churches in most regions of the zone (North Rhine/Westphalia, Lower Saxony, Schleswig Holstein), Bell saw it as of the utmost importance that all policy with the German churches should be coordinated at the headquarters of the Religious Affairs Branch in Bünde. As each of the Religious Commissioners acquired 'religious advisers', they regarded them as on their staff and responsible to the Regional Headquarters. This, as Bell saw quite clearly, could have led to chaos in the delicate matter of Religious Affairs. He did not quite succeed with Berlin which retained the religious adviser within the Educational system. But the extent of his success throughout the Zone can be seen in the proposal of the Religious Affairs Branch, which was eventually accepted:

> "As regards British Control, this is maintained by the Regional Commissioners after seeking the advice of the Regional Religious Affairs Officer. All matters of general policy will be communicated to the Regional Commissioners by or on behalf of the Deputy Military Governor, after consultation with his Religious Affairs adviser [i.e., the Controller of the RA Branch]. The Regional Religious Affairs Officer will keep in close touch with Religious Affairs Headquarters, to which he will refer for guidance in the implementation of general policy."[7]

These issues may seem trivial at this point, as was Bell's strong argument for the RA Controller to be a Brigadier rather than a Colonel! But they were important in a Military/Civil Service structure. Bell succeeded in getting status for the RA Branch. That meant the churches could get the help they needed.

One final step was taken after a visit of a group of British theologians in 1947. Among Bell's papers in Lambeth is a recommendation about the type of people needed in the RA Branch. All had spoken kindly of those they met but R. J. C. Gutteridge (a long time authority on the German churches) wrote a confidential report on 12th December 1947:

> "As regards 'Religious Affairs' Dept., while the highest praise should be given on the way in which some of the officers carry out their work, there is little evidence that much effort has been made to find men for the work who possess a real understanding of both the past and the present religious situation with its complicated theological background. If a really suitable person could be found, I would strongly recommend the appointment of a theological expert on the Religious Affairs staff who could have only the minimum of administrative duties and would therefore have ample time to study the various developments of theological thought and become acquainted with the relevant religious literature."[8]

The proposal was not accepted but the idea was already in Bell's mind and, in cooperation with Aubrey, he had taken some care in recommending the next generation of staff at the RA Branch from 1947 onwards.

The Hamburg Refugee Conference

In 1949 there was a fruitful collaboration with the World Council of Churches in Geneva. The Department of "Inter-Church Aid and Service to Refugees" applied to the British Foreign Office (German Section) for permission to convene a Refugee Conference in Hamburg. This was the brain-child of Elfan Rees, who was then responsible for the WCC's "Service to Refugees". The Foreign Office agreed after consultation with the Religious Affairs Branch and appointed its Acting Head as the official co-organiser. The Conference was held in February 1949 and brought before the Allied and German leaders the task of integrating refugees into political and economic life. Immediately after the Hamburg Conference which had clearly defined the problem, Elfan Rees and I flew to Berlin with a request to General Clay, the Military Governor of the American Zone of Occupation. The reception was not cordial! "So you are the people who want to solve the problems in the British Zone with American money", he said. We had asked for quadripartite funds generated from Marshall Aid to be used for internal rehabilitation of refugees. The intervention of the Bishop of Chichester ensured that, despite General Clay, such funds could be used for the German refugees and, for the first time, the international aspect of this responsibility was accepted! George Bell never gave up! A similar Conference at Salzburg in January 1950 dealt with *Volksdeutsche* (Expellees of German ethnic origin) and displaced persons in Austria, offering them the possibility of a new way of life. George Bell lived up to his reputation as "Champion of the claims of international and social justice", as the World Council of Churches persuaded the world to accept responsibility for the refugees of war, regardless of their origin. It must be remembered that at that time the High Commissioner for Refugees in Germany had to exclude from his mandate refugees of German origin.

After some very useful work the Branch was becoming redundant and even George Bell who had fought for it saw that its days were over. Gerhard Leibholz's recommendation that as soon as possible Germans should control their own life was becoming evident. Most judgements on the Religious Affairs Branch recognised that a difficult job was accomplished with some very positive results. Espez Camp, a former poison gas factory or store, became a centre for youth vocational training by the Churches, instead of being destroyed. St. Michael's House in Blankanese, Hamburg, dealt effectively with youth who had been indoctrinated with Nazi ideology. The German Churches were given the resources they needed. Several smaller religious groups attained their freedom after Nazi oppression. The churches de-Nazified themselves rather more effectively than other parts of German life. In what was in general an unsuccessful 'occupation' the RA Branch did as good a job as any despite the evident weaknesses. That the work was as good as it was is due in no small measure to the diligence of George Bell.

The Assessment of the Occupation

When Bell visited Germany in October 1945, he noted with pain the condition of some of his friends who had suffered at the hands of the Nazis, and from deprivation. One person he mentions is Hans Asmussen, a leading figure in the Confessing Church and one who suffered much in 1942 in a concentration camp. Bell comments briefly "Asmussen had sunken eyes after imprisonment, body sick, spirit alive". Such a man had a right to speak of conditions in Germany under the occupation. He expressed himself strongly in a letter to the Archbishop of Canterbury, comparing the behaviour of the occupying powers to that of the Nazis. The British Delegation of churchmen in 1946 was asked to use what influence it could to mitigate the conditions in the Soviet Zone, but Asmussen also spoke of the British Zone in the strongest language.[9]

There was undoubtedly reprehensible behaviour among the army and the civilian administration. Bell did not miss this on his visit. Had he remained until Christmas he might have been more disturbed by the effect of tax-free liquor at the festive season. The British had little experience of occupying a European country. There was constant complaint about the quality and experience of those recruited for the Control Commission. They were often ex-soldiers and when their wives came to join them they were given a standard of living they were not accustomed to. Many had never had servants before and did not know how to treat the Germans whom they employed in domestic work. Bob Crossett of the BBC Forces Network, referred to them as 'temporary gentlemen'. The tendency among some was to feel that any German who spoke up and disagreed with the military government was arrogant. All this was true and British churchmen as well as the Bishops' wives who visited on the occasion of the Lambeth Conference in 1948 commented upon these abuses. Both France and America chose their personnel more carefully. But this was not the whole picture. After the relaxing of the 'non-fraternisation' order, which forbade social contact between British and Germans, many fast friendships were made. It may not be the majority but certainly a large number at the Control Commission learned to appreciate the strong qualities of the Germans who endured the hardships of occupation.

One example is the Controller of the Religious Affairs Branch, John Gwynne, writing to Karl Barth over the Marahrens affair. He said:

"I cannot help feeling that now when we emerge from the security of Geneva or England where we were at liberty to fulminate against Hitler with impunity it has been all too easy for us to tell them now what they should have done, but I, for my part, having lived out here for over a year, am not able to condemn them for not having done it. On the contrary, I honour and admire many of them for what they did do and I consider they are entitled to some respect and consideration. You yourself, Professor, have been freely urging cooperation with the Bolsheviks, but if there were a war with Russia now and the enemies of Bolshevism won, might not you yourself find yourself in a similar position to that in which Dr. Marahrens was in 1945? In such circumstances I hope no one in a similar position to that in which I now am would try to disgrace and humilate you. I hope that you will understand that I say this with the greatest respect."[10]

George Bell was amused by that comparison, because he had said similar things in his 'Letter to my Friends in the Evangelical Church in Germany'

(14th February 1946). There he took up the words of the Pope's Christmas message,

> "Who can say 'I am free from sin'? Those who exact today the expiation of crimes and the just punishment of criminals for misdeeds should take good care not to do themselves what they denounce in others as misdeeds or crimes."[11]

Bell took the specific example of the refugees from the Eastern provinces:

> "To give the most obvious and vivid illustration – how can the victors, who have so constantly condemned the mass deportations of the civilian populations of both the Western and the Eastern countries by the German government, refuse to condemn mass deportations of millions of Germans from the East into a reduced Germany, or reconcile such notions by any nation with the principles of humanity?"[12]

Notes

1. Klaus Scholder, *Requiem for Hitler*, SCM Press, 1989, pp. 157–167.
2. Gerhard Besier, *"Selbstreinigung" unter britischer Besatzungsherrschaft* ('Self-Cleansing' under the British Occupation), Vandenhoeck & Ruprecht, 1986.
3. *Ibid.*, pp. 199–201.
4. *Ibid.*, pp. 367–371.
5. *Ibid.*, pp. 281–283.
6. *Ibid.*, p. 43.
7. *Ibid.*, p. 47.
8. *Ibid.*, p. 49.
9. Among papers in *Evangelisches Archivzentral*, Berlin.
10. Gerhard Besier, *op. cit.*, pp. 367–368.
11. Bell, *The Church and Humanity*, pp. 190–191.
12. *Ibid.*, p. 191.

10 War Criminals

After six years of war, there was inevitably much bitterness and a demand for punishment. The victors alone could insist upon judgement, but this put any trial for war crimes in question. The Pope had asked pointedly, "Who can say 'I am free from sin'?" George Bell went further in spelling that out in terms of National Socialism itself. He had never hesitated to condemn the Nazis and he accepted that the Germans bore the greatest guilt. But he also added in his "A Letter to my Friends in the Evangelical Church in Germany":

> "Justice, however, demands, and faith in God and hope for the future demands that we who are not Germans should confess our guilt in this fearful common catastrophe. Not to go further back, we in Britain have displayed a criminal levity with regard to our obligation to defend order and peace, and, if the Germans have been intolerably passive in resisting the rise of the Führer, there was a passiveness hardly less conspicuous or less open to reproach on the part of ourselves and other nations, and condoned by our Churches, as we watched the National Socialist system get its stranglehold on the life of Germany, and were too careless, or too late to take the military precautions necessary for Europe's freedom. Although no man's guilt goes so deep as the guilt of Hitler and Himmler no party, no Church, no university is free from some responsibility for the doom which has come upon us."[1]

That was on 14th February 1946. George Bell had heard the Stuttgart Confession of Guilt and the victorious Allies were already conducting the Nuremberg Trials of war criminals. The Nuremberg Charter, however, as he pointed out later (House of Lords, 5th May, 1949) 'dealt only with the crimes of the vanquished'.

The Setting of the Nuremberg Trials

There was nothing new in victorious Allies condemning and punishing those they had conquered. After the First World War, it was the intention to put the Kaiser on trial. He escaped to neutral Netherlands. The Versailles Treaty, however, exacted the punishment without trial. This century has seen consistent efforts to legalise war and war trials. The Hague Convention of 1907 set out the legal requirements for starting a war – 'a reasoned declaration of war' or 'an ultimatum with conditional declaration of war'. Britain came into the Second World War on the latter of these alternatives. The Geneva Prisoners of War and Red Cross Convention of 1929 laid down rules for the treatment of prisoners and care of the sick and wounded. However, neither of these treaties specified how they were to be enforced nor what sanctions should be applied against violation.

After the First World War, the Allied Powers drew up a list of forty-five persons considered guilty of breaking 'customary international law'. Twelve of these were tried by the German Government before the Supreme Court of Leipzig. Only six were convicted. It had been the custom for those charged to be tried in the country where their crimes had been committed. The crimes which the Allies wished to confront after the Second World War could not be identified with any particular country. Some would have had to stand trial in as many as 23 countries. Therefore, acting on behalf of the United Nations (that is the 23 countries who had been at war with Germany), the four major powers, Britain, the USA, France and the USSR, met and negotiated a Charter for an International Tribunal. The agreement, signed in London, on 8th August 1945 was called the 'London Agreement' and it was decided that six trials would be in one place. Twenty-four Nazis and six organisations were named for trial and there were four main counts on the indictment:

"1. The crime of being party to a common plan or conspiracy to wage aggressive war.

2. Crimes against peace – planning, preparing, initiating or waging a war of aggression – or a war in violation of international treaties.

3. War crimes – violation of the laws or customs of war, which included wanton destruction and the mistreatment of prisoners of war.

4. Crimes against humanity – inhuman treatment of civilians, extermination and persecution on racial or religious grounds."

The Russians wanted the trials held in Berlin, but the Americans won the day with their proposal for a town in their zone of occupation: Nuremberg. It was a clever choice. The beautiful medieval town of Nuremberg had been the scene of the greatest Nazi triumphs and was now in ruins. The Court House (The Palace of Justice) and prison, at the west of the town, were intact and these were available for the world trial of Nazi criminals. The court room was large enough to hold people and there were hundreds of offices for lawyers and staff of the four prosecuting nations.

The Nuremberg Trial

At 10 am on the 20th November 1945, the judges, all in black except for the Russians who insisted upon military uniform, filed into their seats before the flags of their four nations. From that day until 31st August 1946 the tribunal sat five or five-and-a-half days every week with only short recesses over the official holiday periods. Each defendant had been given a copy in German of the charges which ran to 24,000 words. Each defendant was allowed to answer to the charges and choose a lawyer to conduct his defence. Judgement was delivered on 30th September and 1st October 1946. Three of the twenty-four indicted did not stand trial. Robert Ley had committed suicide. Gustav Krupp was dismissed because of senility. Martin Bormann was tried *in absentia*. (No one knew whether or not he had died with Hitler in the Berlin Bunker – he was his deputy.) The trial was conducted in four languages with simultaneous translations. Outside, the Palace of Justice was guarded by American tanks, because there was some fear of an SS raid to rescue the accused. The eyes of the world were fixed upon twenty-one men.

The trial has been challenged, not only by George Bell, politically, legally, and regarding the people who were tried. More than a generation later, Klaus Scholder spoke to a mass meeting of young Germans attending the Nuremberg *Kirchentag* in 1979 on the place of Nuremberg in history. He gave a fair assessment of 'what this unparalleled trial achieved and what it did not'.[2] What it achieved he said was considerable and he listed three points:

1. This Trial was not a show trial, but in fact an open, legal hearing. There may be many legal questions, but the accused were able to defend themselves and the judges were determined that justice should be done. One has only to remember the alternatives proposed in Teheran in 1943. Stalin had proposed shooting 50,000 or even 100,000 German officers without trial. In America, Morgenthau called for the immediate execution of the main known Nazis without trial.

2. Because it was a court sitting through forty-two volumes of evidence, 'parts of the truth about the Third Reich came to light which would not otherwise have been believed'. The trial attempted to get at the truth and after all the criticisms of it have been made, 'one can no longer argue about the criminal character of National Socialism'. Even the accused learned things about National Socialism which they had not known and as the trial went on became more and more ashamed. Only a few of the accused were convinced Nazis at the end.

F. T. Grossmith, who was sent as chaplain to the accused wrote to his wife:

"Another day with the men upon whom all the world set its eyes, and most for condemnation. Well, maybe so, but there's something going on inside their hearts since I have been seeing them that can only be measured in spiritual value."[3]

Some have accused Nuremberg of depriving the Germans of the opportunity of sitting in judgement on the sins of their fellow-countrymen themselves. Anyone who knew the state of Germany in 1945/1946 knows that that would have been impossible. The Allies did what had to be done and they may be criticised for the way they did it, but there was no one else to do it. They made a first discovery of the truth and their passing judgement has been a contribution to the new beginning which Germany sought after 1945.

But there is something it did not achieve and this the International Court of Justice needed: it had no precedent, but the Allies failed to lay the foundations for a law, making 'aggressive wars, war crimes and crimes against humanity, including genocide, universally recognised criminal actions'.

George Bell and the War Criminals

Klaus Scholder in 1979 gave a much more favourable verdict on the controversial trial than Bell did at the time. This is partly because George Bell had concentrated upon the Churches and the reconstruction of Germany. The World Council of Churches was being prepared and Marc Boegner, Head of the Protestant Church in France and Father of the World Council of Churches, saw Bell as his successor. When George Bell discussed the Nuremberg Trial with him, they both agreed that it should not drag on too long, but for quite different reasons. Marc Boegner was of the opinion that those who had to wait for sentence usually got off lightly.

Bell felt that it was cruel to continue these trials too long and later advocated that the aged offenders should be set free. He persistently, though unsuccessfully, urged the release of Rudolf Hess.

In 1947, two publications appeared which greatly supported Bell's point of view. Montgomery Belgion wrote a pamphlet called *Epitaph on Nuremberg* and Professor H. A. Smith published *Crisis in the Law of Nations*. Smith was particularly important because of the role he had played in the 'Belsen Trials'. He did not minimise the awful atrocities of Belsen, but he found the trial illegal and therefore unjust. Bell discussed the matter with Gerhard Leibholz and then arranged to meet H. A. Smith in June 1948. (As a result he spoke out in the House of Lords, 23rd June 1948).

In January 1949, he told Lord Henderson, who was then at the Foreign Office, that he wanted to raise the question in the House of Lords of releasing Admiral Raeder, who was now 74, and Baron von Neurath who was 77. He was not given time until 5th May 1949 when he spoke at length. He argued that the prolongation of the trials was inhuman and that the Nuremberg Charter was open to serious criticisms. He had three charges against the Nuremberg Trial:

1. Only the vanquished were tried – had the victors committed no crimes?
2. The view that a war of aggression is a crime against peace is disputed in international law.
3. A man acting under superior orders is not responsible for the crimes he commits.

It was typical of Bell that after dealing with legal niceties he should go at once to the humanitarian argument. The conditions in Spandau he said were appalling. He used language similar to that he had used about the treatment of internees during the war. He asked for a review of the sentences of all war criminals who had already been sentenced, and no more trials. Three of the original accused were still awaiting trial four years after the opening of the process in Nuremberg: Field Marshal von Runstedt, Field Marshal von Manstein and General Strauss. They had waited four years in prison. All three were now over sixty and all three suffering from ill health. He asked that they be freed.[4] Lord Henderson answered that Field Marshal von Manstein had been declared fit to stand trial. He would be the last. Further names, he said, would be handed over to the German courts to deal with themselves. Lord Henderson also asserted that conditions in Spandau had improved. Through his questioning in the House of Lords Bell discovered an ally – Lord Hankey, who had disagreed with the proposed trials as early as 1943. Hankey was at that time a member of the War Cabinet. Now he was trying to get the wartime Foreign Minister of Japan released. Bell and Hankey made common cause and constantly approached the government about the release of war criminals.

The Influence of the World Council of Churches

The World Council of Churches, for many years 'in process of formation', was constituted at an assembly in Amsterdam in 1948. On Sunday, 22nd August at 8 pm the delegates of 147 churches assembled for the opening session of the First Assembly of the World Council of Churches. For George Bell it was a thrilling moment when the hopes and prayers of years were fulfilled. On the Monday morning, 23rd August 1948, Marc Boegner submitted the following resolution in the name of the Committee of Fourteen and the Provincial Committee:

"That the First Assembly of the World Council of Churches be declared to be and is hereby constituted in accordance with the Constitution drafted at Utrecht in 1938 and approved by the Churches: that the Assembly consists of those persons who have been appointed as the official delegates of the Churches adhering to the Council; and that the formation of the World Council of Churches be declared and is hereby completed."[5]

That was accepted without dissent, but on the understanding that the Constitution of twenty years before could be amended, and it was, a week later. The World Council of Churches was born and it carried the slogan, "We intend to stay together".

The Assembly approved the setting up of a Central Committee of 90 members to take policy decisions during the five-year periods between Assemblies. That Committee was representative of the participating Confessions from 30 nations and included 15 lay people. The Central Committee was expected to meet annually and between those meetings an Executive Committee elected from its number would meet to deal with urgent matters. The Chairman of both Committees was George Bell.

As was to be expected Bell was on the Message Committee once again and it is not difficult to trace his influence on much of its wording. The Committee was a large one under the chairmanship of the Bishop of Oslo, Dr. Eivind Berggrav, and was representative of many countries and traditions. From Germany, there were two – Martin Niemöller and Edmund Schlink, both active in the Confessing Church. Martin had led the Confessing Church, but from 1937 had been in prison. Edmund Schlink had served in many capacities and in 1946 he became Professor for Dogmatic and Ecumenical Theology at Heidelberg. He was 45 at the time of Amsterdam and his ecumenical involvement continued until he died in 1984. Many of Bell's friends were on that Committee, colleagues with whom he had worked for unity in the inter-war years. Apart from the German members, Bell had a special interest in Josef Hromadka, who had tried to cooperate with the Communist government in his native Czechoslovakia.

Bishop Berggrav presented the Message to the General Meeting of the Assembly. He described it as 'like a pastoral letter to fellow-Christians and a symbol of the fellowship in Christ now felt all over the world'. Bishop Lesslie Newbigin then read the Message in English, Pastor Pierre Maury read it in French, Pastor Niemöller in German.

The Message of the First Assembly of the World Council of Churches

"The World Council of Churches, meeting at Amsterdam, sends this message of greeting to all who are in Christ, and to all who are willing to hear.

"We bless God our Father and our Lord Jesus Christ, Who gathers together in one the children of God that are scattered abroad. He has brought us here together in Amsterdam. We are one in acknowledging Him as our God and Saviour. We are divided from one another not only in matters of faith, order and tradition, but also by pride of nation, class and race. But Christ has made us his own, and He is not divided. In seeking Him we find one another. Here at Amsterdam we have committed ourselves afresh to Him, and have covenanted with one another in constituting this World Council of Churches. We intend to stay together. We call upon Christian congregations everywhere to endorse and fulfil this covenant in their relations one with another. In thankfulness to God we commit the future to Him.

"When we look to Christ, we see the world as it is – His world, to which He came and for which He died. It is filled both with great hopes and also with disillusionment and despair. Some nations are rejoicing in new freedom and power, some are bitter because freedom is denied them, some are paralysed by division, and everywhere there is an undertone of fear. There are millions who are hungry, millions who have no home, no country and no hope. Over all mankind hangs the peril of total war. We have to accept God's judgement upon us for our share in the world's guilt. Often we have tried to serve God and Mammon, put other loyalties before loyalty to Christ, confused the Gospel with our own economic or national or racial interests, and feared war more than we have hated it. As we have talked with each other here, we have begun to understand how our separation has prevented us from receiving correction from one another in Christ. And because we lacked this correction, the world had often heard from us not the Word of God but the words of men.

"But there is a Word of God for our world. It is that the world is in the hands of the living God, Whose will for it is wholly good; that in Christ Jesus, His incarnate Word, Who lived and died and rose from the dead, God has broken the power of evil once for all, and opened for everyone the gate into freedom, and joy in the Holy Spirit; that the final judgement on all human history and on every human deed is the judgement of the merciful Christ; and that the end of history will be the triumph of His Kingdom, where alone we shall understand how much God has loved the world. This is God's unchanging Word to the world. Millions of our fellow-men have never heard it. As we are met here from many lands, we pray God to stir up His whole Church to make this Gospel known to the whole world, and to call on all men to believe in Christ, to live in His love and to hope for His coming.

"Our coming together to form a World Council will be vain unless Christians and Christian congregations everywhere commit themselves to the Lord of the Church in a new effort to seek together, where they live, to be His witnesses and servants among their neighbours. We have to remind ourselves and all men that God has put down the mighty from their seats and exalted the humble and meek. We have to learn afresh together to speak boldly in Christ's name both to those in power and to the people, to oppose terror, cruelty and race discrimination, to stand by the outcast, the prisoner and the refugee. We have to make of the Church in every place a voice for those who have no voice, and a home where every man will be at home. We have to learn afresh together what is the duty of the Christian man or woman in industry, in agriculture, in politics, in the professions and in the home. We have to ask God to teach us together to say 'No' and to say 'Yes' in truth. 'No', to all that flouts the love of Christ, to every system, every programme and every person that treats any man as though he were an irresponsible thing or a means of profit, to the defenders of injustice in the name of order, to those who sow the seeds of war or urge war as inevitable; 'Yes', to all that conforms to the love of Christ, to all who seek for justice, to the peacemakers, to all who hope, fight and suffer for the cause of man, to all who – even without knowing it – look for new heavens and a new earth wherein dwelleth righteousness.

"It is not in man's power to banish sin and death from the earth, to create the unity of the Holy Catholic Church, to conquer the hosts of Satan. But it is within the power of God. He has given us at Easter the certainty that His purpose will be accomplished. But, by our acts of obedience and faith, we can on earth set up signs which point to the coming victory. Till the day of that victory our lives are hid with Christ in God, and no earthly disillusion or distress or power of hell can separate us from Him. As those who wait in confidence and joy for their deliverance, let us give ourselves to those tasks which lie to our hands, and so set up signs that men may see.

"Now unto Him that is able to do exceeding abundantly above all that we ask or think, according to the power that worketh in us, unto Him be glory in the Church by Christ Jesus, throughout all ages, world without end."[6]

When that document is laid beside the reports of the long drawn-out Nuremberg Trial it is not difficult to see how Bell could persuade the World Council of Churches whose staff was in Geneva, that actions should be taken to see that sentences could be reviewed. The World Council could work through its members to persuade governments to adopt a common and enlightened policy. Bell's attitude is well summed up in a letter to Liddell Hart, which is preserved in the Lambeth Palace Library, dated 9th March 1950, shortly after a meeting in Geneva with the WCC staff and some Committee Members including Marc Boegner:

"The upshot of a fairly long discussion was a general agreement, that everywhere there should be reconsideration, and that the whole business had gone on far too long, further that individual members of our committee should take up the matter personally with their own governments, and that we should try to get a common agreement as to the policy asked for. A small group convened by the Swiss Professor Courvoisier and including myself, is engaged in drawing up a brief statement of the kind of policy *viz.* no more extradition, review of all sentences and of all trials."[7]

Success

In 1949, George Bell had been Bishop of Chichester for twenty years. Those who knew him in his youth foretold a brilliant career. He had all the contacts and he was above average intelligence and ability. Randall Davidson regarded him as indispensable. He was early at a Lambeth Conference, even before he was a Bishop. In 1929, when he became Bishop of Chichester, he was only forty-six. He might reasonably expect that in the course of time he would be offered a more important role – London, perhaps – and surely one day, Archbishop of Canterbury. If the Germans had had a vote they would certainly have elected him to the highest office. He rapidly gained international experience, he was a brilliant organiser, he could negotiate and draft policy statements. Perhaps his ecumenical involvement was a bit excessive for some. But the main obstacle to his preferment was obviously his unflinching honesty. His sense of what was right and just was absolute and he could not trim. Popular movements did not sway him – either in Germany or in England. He saw the evil of National Socialism when others were trying to adjust to it. He applied moral standards to the conduct of war and he could not keep quiet when something had to be said. His battle for the war criminals was completely unintelligible to many. Surely, he had denounced the evils of the Nazis. Why was he defending these monsters? The horrors of Auschwitz were out and no treatment was too severe for those who had been responsible. They did not deserve justice. The nation worked itself up into a frenzy of hatred against these men on trial. They deserved no sympathy and no quarter. Bell saw old men in prison for four years still waiting for their trial and worked for humanity. This gentle bishop with no ambition for himself loved his Church and honoured his position as Lord Spiritual in the House of Lords. He was there to place the moral imperative before the Upper House, and he did so without fear or favour. His courage is recorded in *Hansard*, but he was equally outspoken with his Church – both nationally and in his diocese. He had taken up many unpopular causes – the bombing of non-military objectives, the internment of refugees, the German rations in occupied Berlin, even the war criminals. It was not a question of whether they deserved justice, but what it would do to us if we disregarded it.

The United Nations had based the Nuremberg Trial on a law enacted for the purpose and retrospectively applied. The British government was party to that. It was difficult to defend legally however natural it was in the circumstances to exact punishment. Bell could not let that pass and he withstood popular disapproval and official malice. He liked people and did not enjoy being reproached or passed over. But his principles remained resolute. If an action was wrong or inhuman it had to be resisted. He did not give up. Although constantly advised not to raise the issue that troubled his conscience, he was prepared to wait, but not to be silent. And if his courage is recorded in *Hansard*, so are his successes.

On 1st November 1951, in answer to a question by Bell on the fate of those awaiting trial in Berlin, the Leader of the House of Lords, Lord Salisbury, assured him that the matter was being sympathetically considered. Lord Hankey had also pressed and Salisbury assured him that it was under active consideration and would form part of the negotiations with the German government due soon. This happened and it was possible to announce that Adenauer, then German Chancellor, agreed to the hastening of the release of the Germans still serving sentence in Germany. Both Bell and Hankey kept pressing until Baron von Neurath, Admiral Raeder and Admiral Donnitz were released from Spandau. Bell persisted still and many lesser 'criminals' were released. Again and again, Bell was worried by the fact that the law under which they were sentenced had been a law invented for the purpose – and retrospective. Jasper sums up Bell's position:

"Bell never denied that there might be a hard core of evil men who deserved their fate: but he was concerned with those who had at the time, broken no existing law by fighting for their country; some had acted under stress and, as they thought – for the best; some were even innocent of the crimes of which they had been falsely accused."[8]

Bell's arguments were controlled by principles which he could not give up. And he would prefer a guilty man to go free rather than an innocent man be convicted. The passions of war are not the best feelings by which to punish the defeated justly – whether they deserved it or not.

Notes

1. G. K. A. Bell, *The Church and Humanity*, p. 190.
2. Klaus Scholder, *Requiem for Hitler*, pp. 15–17.
3. F. T. Grossmith, *The Cross and the Swastika* (private publication), H. E. Walter, Worthing, 1984, p. 54.
4. *Hansard*, House of Lords, 5th May 1949. (*cf.* Jasper, *op. cit.*, pp. 307–308).
5. *The First Assembly of the World Council of Churches: The Official Report*, edited by W. A. Visser 't Hooft, SCM Press, London, 1949, p. 28 (*cf.* Marc Boegner, *The Long Road to Unity*, pp. 219–225).
6. *Ibid.*, pp. 9–11.
7. *The Bell Papers*, Lambeth Palace Library, Letter to Liddell Hart, 9th March 1950, Vol. 38.
8. *Op. cit.*, p. 309.

11   The Soviet Zone:
The German Democratic Republic

As a member of the House of Lords, Bishop Bell's prime concern was with the British Zone of occupation in Germany; but as a member of the Provisional Committee of the World Council of Churches and, from 1948, Chairman of its Central Committee, he was also concerned with conditions in other zones. His visit to Germany had been primarily to the Western Zones in October 1945. His only contact with the Soviet Zone was in Berlin. He saw that there were differences between the Zones, but was unwilling to draw conclusions. The "Russian Zone" he reported, "has its own method of land reform which hits very large numbers of people very hard. But I am bound to say that, because of the mystery which surrounds the Russian Zone there is great fear in the other three Zones". In Berlin he glimpsed something of the state of the the Church in the Soviet Zone when he preached in the *Marienkirche* (see p. 113 above), the principal Protestant Parish Church in the Soviet sector of that divided city. He was then deeply moved, commenting:

> "There was an enormous congregation of people, some standing. There was a real spiritual hunger and expectancy. You felt that any word that could be said of reconciliation and charity and love would fall like balm upon their ears and souls. You wanted to say something to give them hope for the future. In a way they want material things very badly indeed, but still more they want help, spiritual succour and personal friendship."[1]

Delegation of the British Council of Churches to Germany
(28th November to 13th December, 1945)

Even before Bishop Bell made his visit to Germany in October 1945 the British Council of Churches had made a decision to send an official delegation there. This delegation eventually went at the end of November and included W. R. Matthews (Dean of St. Paul's), M. E. Aubrey (General Secretary of the Baptist Union), John Baillie (Principal of New College, Edinburgh) accompanied by Canon H. N. Waddams as interpreter. Bell awaited their report with interest. Among the chief impressions was a clear recognition of the problems caused by the flood of refugees from the East, which led to German pastors being preoccupied with the refugee situation. The last point they made was that:

"The attitude of the Church Leaders to Russia was an embarrassment to us in our conversations, and will almost certainly present difficulties in any future ecumenical collaboration. It is important that this should be clearly recognised. The root of the antagonism of the Church Leaders to Russia is partly the reports which came from the Russian Zone, but chiefly the conviction that the Russians aim at destroying everything that is valuable in Western tradition. It must be borne in mind that the antagonism between Teuton and Slav is very ancient and therefore very deep-seated."[2]

Arthur Cotter of the Control Commission who accompanied the delegation prepared the official report, which Bell saw. He read there a much more detailed account of the delegation's visit to Berlin and, in particular, the long session with Bishop Dibelius, much of whose diocese was in the Soviet Zone. Bell knew Dibelius well and how reliable he was too. So what he read filled him with dismay:

"The Bishop began the interview by describing the conditions in East Prussia and Pomerania, where thousands of Germans were still living. [By the Potsdam Agreement these territories were officially annexed to Poland and the Soviet Union.] The worst conditions, he said, prevailed in Polish Pomerania. Evangelical Churches were seized and reconsecrated as Roman Catholic churches. Nobody was allowed to enter the area and they learned of conditions from those who were driven out. Transport was frightful. In Mecklenburg [still retained as German, but in the Soviet Zone of Occupation] alone there had arrived from East Prussia 400,000 Germans. The civil administration had issued an order that the population must care for these people. There were no dwellings available so they were preparing cattle stalls and digging holes in the ground for them to live in. More were to come in January and February. The people were being literally driven out, although they were made to sign a form to the effect that they left voluntarily. It was a migration of people amounting to eight or ten million. The Polish government, he said, was in a position to control this migration but did not want to do so. Instead the Germans were given orders to leave, sometimes within ten minutes. The trains were guarded by Polish Militia who disappeared when the marauders came and plundered them, so that they arrived on German soil with nothing at all and nearly all sick."[3]

Dibelius was Bishop of Berlin and Brandenburg, which made him, as he said, "the Presiding Bishop of the Soviet Zone". The report he gave of conditions under Russian control was bleak in the extreme. Cotter's report also contains summaries of the accounts given by others who knew of conditions in the Soviet Zone at first hand – Dr. Knak, Secretary of the German Missionary Council, and Pastor Lokies, Director of the Gossner Mission. Lokies pointed out that East Germany was in a process of impoverishment. The Churches had lost all their funds and what was worse still was that among their young people in Greifswald, Jena and Leipzig were hardly any theological students. "The young men who wanted to study and were strong crossed the frontier by secret routes and the same held true of the professors". The Church in the Soviet Zone was facing a breakdown, according to Dr. Knak, but Dibelius still believed that a religious awakening would come from the East. "God's way led the German Church into scarcity and catastrophe, but gave anew a strong inner life". The factual reporting, however, was hard for Bell to read without deep concern:

> "The German Church in the Soviet Zone was facing a breakdown. The clergy were paid neither stipends nor pensions and were utterly impoverished, but that gave rise to a greater readiness to sacrifice. The Russians did not understand such organisations as the YMCA and the *Frauenhilfe* [women's work]. The Russians had given the power to the Communist Party which was, in Germany, a minority party and the Communists endeavoured in every way to hinder the work of the Church, so that they were in constant struggle with the Communist Burgomasters."[4]

Despite this the majority of the clergy wished to stay where they were. Very few sought to move to the West. The British Council of Churches delegation did not visit the Soviet Zone, except for Berlin, but news was coming out of the zone in addition to the evidence from the condition of the expellees, which was most disturbing.

Reinhold von Thadden-Trieglaff

One of the most distinguished lay leaders in the Church of Pomerania was a soldier and landowner who had been Commander of the German Army in Louvain, Belgium. There he had used his authority to keep the Gestapo out and governed Louvain in a civilised way. So much so that he was honoured after the war with the freedom of the city! When his troops were ordered to retreat before the advancing British Army he refused to destroy, as ordered, the stores that the army could not take with them, but distributed them among the hungry population of Louvain. He retired as the war ended to his estates in Pomerania, was present when the Nazis executed his sister and was arrested by the Communists. He was never a Nazi, but the Russians could not believe that. He was treated in a barbaric way which ruined his health and left him with a broken voice. Nonetheless, he led the *Kirchentag* (annual Church Rally) movement, after the war with remarkable success. When he was at his lowest he tells of a Polish companion who rescued him from despair:

> "There I lay, feverish and growing weaker, without the will to live, more and more like so many of my fellow prisoners who died because they had no resistance left. A Polish companion dragged me out of this lethargy. He came to see me frequently, squatted by my bed and insisted, 'You must eat'. I answered, 'I can't eat', but I did manage to eat a little bread and swallow a few mouthfuls of soup. Then he said, 'You mustn't lie here all the time. You must get up'. I said, 'I can't stand', and yet in the end he got me on my feet. Then he said, 'You must go out into the fresh air'. I said, 'I can't walk', but he got hold of me, held me up, and got me outside the barracks. So it was that my life was saved for the third time. This time by a Pole."[5]

Werner Hühne who records that incident in his biography of Reinhold von Thadden-Trieglaff, *A Man to be Reckoned With*, describes the experience of many others. "Thousands of German men and women endured similar experiences during the collapse of the Nazi regime. They perished on the miserable journey to Siberia or in the forced labour camps in the measureless Russian wastes". The fact that Thadden's health was permanently impaired, that his nose was broken by a soldier's rifle butt and remained deformed, that his voice never regained its strength was simply 'sharing the fate of thousands'." Such stories reached the West and led Churchill to speak of an 'Iron Curtain' dividing Europe between East and West, when addressing an American audience in Fulton, Missouri, 6th March 1946.

The Visit of Sylvester C. Michelfelder
(3rd November–15th December 1945)

Bell had to read an even more distressing report from his colleagues of the Lutheran World Federation. Michelfelder was an American Lutheran. His visit to Germany with a team of American Lutherans included going to a receiving centre in Berlin organised by *Evangelische Hilfswerk* (Church Social Work) administered by Probst Grüber. The description of the plight of those who had drifted westwards, harassed with every indignity on the way, was horrific – "the sight which met our eyes will never be forgotten and we were told that this was one of the best in Berlin". They heard that there were thirteen to sixteen million people moving westwards but figures were sheer guesswork. The suffering was not. It demonstrates the cruelty of revenge regardless of guilt. They were told that eight hundred thousand people were living in caves. "If help does not come to these people or if the Russian and Polish and Czechoslovakian governments do not cease this deportation", Michelfelder wrote, "it is quite likely that 90% of these people will die". He was also able to give some account of the condition of the churches in the Soviet Zone gleaned from those who had escaped:

> "Under the new policy of land reform the large farmowners must give up their holdings in the Russian occupied territories, all youth activities in the Church are forbidden as well as Inner Mission and *Hilfswerk* help. The Church has also lost its finances. It is estimated that about 150 million marks have been confiscated. It is true that the Russians keep freedom of worship but by that they mean only the formal part of worship. They do not mean preaching. Saxony seems to be most influenced by communism and it was said that the German Communists are worse than the Russian Communists in the effect upon the Church. Nazism and Bolshevism seem to be about the same because in both the state is everything."[6]

Stewart Herman's Visit from Geneva

About the same time Stewart Herman, who made frequent visits into Germany from Geneva, talked with Bishop Meiser of Bavaria and learned that in order to make room for two or three million expected from Czechoslovakia, Hungary and Yugoslavia, those who had fled from the Soviet Zone were compelled to return. This applied particularly to those people from Thuringia and Saxony who had come to Bavaria during the war. They were in despair because they were going back to nothing with nothing.

Martin Onnasch

In a special issue of *Kirchliche Zeitgeschichte* (1989, I), Martin Onnasch, who has made a study of the Church in the DDR, summarised the situation as it developed 1945–1949:

> "Before the occupation zones were finally established in August 1945, the Soviet occupation power licensed political parties and installed an administration managed by Germans

[overwhelmingly communist]. Within these structures, the Churches were enabled to collaborate. Attempts were made to reform the Church, but because of the extreme stress under which pastors had to work with their immense load, the traditional structures were left more or less intact. In the course of a few years, the attempts at collaboration between church and state in public life turned into confrontation with the pro-communist party on criteria and methods of social transformation in the zone. One disappointment was the failure of the Church in the Soviet Zone to continue what had been learned in the Church Struggle with Nazism, namely the deep concentration upon the biblical word. So that which had sustained the Confessing Church under Hitler no longer did so effectively under communism. The political and ethical challenges presented by a Soviet occupation were not mastered." (English Summary)[7]

The Church lost control of the schools and soon the secular confirmation services made inroads into the youth work. But this did not last.

George Bell was concerned with these changes, but more particularly at first he was involved in the problems of those expelled from the lost provinces. He quickened the work of the "Inter-Church Aid and Service to Refugees" Department of the World Council of Churches. From 1950, however, he directed his attention to what the Russian Occupation was doing to the Churches.

World Council of Churches

In January 1950, when Dean Halfdan Hoegsbrø of Sweden was due to visit the western zones on behalf of the WCC, Bell suggested to him that he might seek an interview with Wilhelm Pieck, President of the German Democratic Republic [the Soviet Zone of Occupation]. The issues for discussion would be the spiritual oversight of German workers in Russia (mostly prisoners of war), the repatriation of Germans from Poland and Czechoslovakia, and an amnesty for Germans serving sentences of forced labour in Siberia (mostly since the end of the war or earlier). With the help of Probst Grüber and Bishop Dibelius, Hoegsbrø was given permission to visit the Soviet Zone and met with Wilhelm Pieck and Herr Nuschke, the Minister in Charge of Church Affairs. Grüber accompanied Hoegsbrø and they were received cordially. Dean Hoegsbrø explained the nature of the WCC and its concern for the spiritual welfare of the German Churches without interfering in politics. The President replied that the

German Churches in the Eastern Zone 'had full opportunity to cooperate with the World Council'. Then Hoegsbrø asked 'if a representative of the World Council could get permanent permission to enter the zone'. Both Pieck and Nuschke were quite positive about this and said this should be possible. It was a good interview, but nothing came of it.

Bell received a report of the interview and the hoped-for permission and wrote to General Archibald at the Religious Affairs Branch of the British Control Commission. He asked for his support to establish a World Council of Churches' representative, who should live in Berlin and be accessible to all parts of Germany. Martin Niemöller gave his support to this and it was generally assumed that the representative would not be American, British or French, but possibly from Sweden or some part of Scandinavia.

General Archibald was cautious in his reply. He wrote on 3rd February 1950 that while the heads of the Religious Affairs Branch were sympathetic with the intentions, there were provisos – 'provided it did not lead to political complications', 'provided it was not wrongly exploited in certain quarters for propaganda purposes'. He also thought that because of the 'critical situation between Eastern and Western Germany' the proposal and the reaction of the German Democratic Republic could not be taken at face value. It was clear that the British Control Commission was not very happy about the presence of a representative of the World Council of Churches in Berlin, probably a neutral, who had free access to all zones!

In February 1950, there was little trust between the occupying powers of East and West, and in none of the zones was there 'open government'. General Archibald was no doubt instructed to register 'apprehension'.[8]

Although West Germany had an Occupation Statute, had held an Election in 1948 and was now an independent state – a *Bundesrepublik* (a Federal Republic) – and the Soviet Zone was now an independent republic, the *DDR* (German Democratic Republic), Berlin was still governed by the four occupying powers jointly and there was no peace treaty yet. All four suspected each other of taking propaganda advantages and it is difficult to discover who exactly turned down the proposal. All that can be said is that 'it failed to secure general acceptance'.

Freedom of Religion in East Germany

That part of Germany which passed under Soviet control is the most Lutheran and, in many ways, the most German part of the country. It is the land where Martin Luther sparked off the Reformation, where Bach lived and composed, where Goethe made his home, where the modern German state first arose out of the discipline and scrupulous honesty of

Friedrich Wilhelm's Prussia, and where cities like Leipzig, Jena, Dresden and Berlin were for a century radiating centres of scholarship and culture. Bell was aware of this when he went to the Wartburg in Eisenach for the second Anglo-German Theological Conference in August 1928. It was there, a year later that, at the meeting of the Stockholm Continuation Committee, he presented a resolution which was one of the most courageous and far-sighted actions that the ecumenical movement has ever taken. It followed on the Treaty of Paris (ie, the Kellog-Briand Pact) condemning recourse to war for the solution of international problems. The crucial part of Bell's resolution was an appeal to the Christian communities in all countries that signed the Treaty of Paris to refuse to support their own country if it went to war without first trying negotiation. Until then Bell had been a silent observer and drafter of messages. In 1929 the newly appointed Bishop of Chichester found a voice in Eisenach.

Twenty years later, he found that very German part of Germany under Soviet control and the witness of the Church weakened further. Bell had many informants, some of whom he had known before the Nazi tragedy. From them he learned of the changing situation. He was not slow in reporting this by whatever means he could. He saw developing in East Germany a conflict between the German Communist Party, backed by the Soviet Union, and the Church, part of which resolutely refused to give up its concern for all the people. Johannes Hamel, who had been trained in the Confessing Church, was a student-pastor at the University of Halle in the DDR. An article by him in 1951 had caused a stir in the Church. Charles West of Geneva translated this and it was read in England. The title must have appealed to Bell: "God's Beloved East Zone". Dr. West pointed out that in this article the four dangers which Hamel's sermons had described as warnings to the Church in the DDR were:

1. The danger of *inner immigration,* the greatest single danger which confronts the Church. This amounts to a withdrawal from all responsible life in the DDR. Against it, Hamel urges an acceptance of the situation. "*This* government in the East, these communist powers, are given to the people of East Germany by God, that they should help them to fulfil the purpose for which he has ordained them".

2. The danger of *fear and hate* – the image of the man with his fist clenched in his pocket is no attitude for a Christian. "God decrees that all men be saved. He commands us to pray for and be subject to them all – even the Communists. Because God is at work we need not fear, and we may not hate."

3. The danger of *idealising the Communist state,* which some have fallen for in one of two ways – either making an amalgam of Marxism and

Christianity, or separating theology from political judgement and analysis.

4. The danger of *conformity* and *nihilism*, which is most marked among young people. Only a few become either activists for the Communist ideology or rebels against it. The majority, torn between home and school, overfed with propaganda, forced into the artificial community of communist youth clubs, give up the search for meaning in life or for values.[9]

Bell was beginning to see the problems of East Germany within the framework of this conflict between Church and State. There were different types of problems. First, and continuing, the increasing number of refugees coming over to western zones. Despite the decision of the Bavarian government to send back those who had come west during the war, the refugees came, both from the 'lost provinces' and from the Soviet Zone. Conditions were much better in the west. Bavaria was in the American Zone, but both types of refugees from the Soviet Zone made their way to Schleswig-Holstein as well and that was in the British Zone. Bell, with his long experience of the refugee problem, was at work gathering aid and appealing for these refugees. The other problems were in the Soviet Zone itself. One was material and he pressed for aid to the Soviet Zone. A response was possible and the giving of aid grew steadily over the years. The other was the conflict in which the churches suffered. They were regarded as aliens and at best vestiges of a primitive past. There was officially freedom to worship; but the whole atmosphere was against the Christians in their daily life. He studied this carefully and strove to keep contact with "God's Beloved East Zone".

The Daily Conflicts under an Atheist Government

Richard W. Solberg, who lived in Germany for the five years that followed upon the end of the war, as Religious Adviser to the US High Commissioner, made a special study of the conditions of Christians in the DDR and reported to Geneva. He also summarised these conditions in his book, *God and Caesar in East Germany*:

> "Some areas of community life could be expected to produce conflicts more readily than others. The Christian layman might, for example, participate with good conscience in an agricultural cooperative or a state-owned factory, and bear a Christian witness through the diligence and excellence of his work. But in view of the ideological character of the schools and of the social law, it would seem very questionable that a person could serve as a teacher or a judge without denying his

Christian faith. In an atheist state, active participation by a Christian in the political process would be exceedingly difficult. Membership in a political party such as the SED [Social Democratic Unity Party], which is committed to an atheist position, would be impossible for an honest and thoughtful Christian. Even the most elementary political act, that of casting a ballot in a general election, the Christian would discover to be fraught with conflicts of conscience. For he would have no choice on election day except to cast his vote for the single slate of hand-picked candidates, all committed in advance to the support of the atheistic principles of the leading political party. The counsel which a Christian pastor, fortified by such a consensus of his colleagues, might give to his inquiring parishioner could never relieve him of his own daily responsibility of decision. No all-inclusive rules can be established to fit every situation and in very few of these situations are the issues black and white."[10]

There is nothing that the World Council of Churches could do about that and it was not unique. In the West too, "the frontier of individual Christian decision is the battle line of the Church". The main action of the WCC was to keep in touch with the churches of the East. In this they were strongly supported by the churches in West Germany. The Evangelical Church in Germany (EKD) insisted as long as it could upon treating Germany as one. The *Kirchentag*, the annual mass lay rally of the Protestant Church in Germany, was for the whole of Germany and it was held in Leipzig one year. Reluctantly it was eventually forced to divide, but even then representatives from East and West went straight to each other's *Kirchentag*, and both retained the custom of entertaining overseas guests.

Political Pressure

Where George Bell could act, however, was in the political field. He had a voice in the House of Lords and his last speech there on 30th January 1958 was an account of further attacks made upon the Church in Eastern Germany. Before then, he had spoken and written often and reminded listeners and readers that three Articles of the Constitution guaranteed freedom of religion in the DDR and he pressed for their fulfilment.

Article 42 guaranteed the right of the Church to administer her affairs independently of the State, and to give shape and order to the religious profession of her members without State interference.

Article 43 guaranteed the right of the Church to organise religious instruction in the State schools.

Article 48 guaranteed the right of parents to decide on their children's religious affiliation up to the age of 15.

These articles were drafted when there was still quadri-partite government. After the split which led to the blockade of Berlin and the Air-Lift, there was little cooperation between the western and eastern occupying forces, except in Berlin. Nonetheless, the Government of the DDR and the leaders of the Evangelical Church signed protocols in 1953 and again in 1956, after periods of disturbance in Berlin and Hungary respectively, reaffirming the guarantees for freedom of religion contained in these three articles. The guarantees were not adhered to and Bell made his protest clearly.

Bell's Retirement from the House of Lords

Bell made his last speech in the House of Lords on 30th January, 1958. Before he could begin, others rose to pay tribute to him as *Hansard* records:

"The EARL of HOME: I think that the speech which we are about to hear from the right reverend Prelate is the last that he will make in your Lordships' House, after twenty-one years of consecutive service on the Bishops' Bench – an honourable record, indeed, and one which I feel must be most unusual. During that time he has been a fearless critic on matters of foreign policy, and he has distributed his rebukes impartially, on all Governments. We have admired his honest, forthright stand on those matters in which he is interested, and we have been stimulated by his criticism. I am sure that the whole House would wish the right reverend Prelate to take with him into retirement our good wishes for his health and happiness."

"Viscount ALEXANDER of HILLSBOROUGH: My Lords, I would heartily endorse the sentiments expressed by the noble Earl the Leader of the House. We have often listened to the right reverend Prelate, and although we have not always agreed with him I have sometimes felt that he has been much nearer to us than to noble Lords opposite. We admire his work in attempting to get religious unity in Europe and for those who are working in Germany for the *Kirchentag*. We in the workers' movement never forget that the right reverend Prelate rendered such service to organised workers that he was made an honorary member of a trade union. I do not know of any other Bishop in your Lordships' House who is in a like position of being able to say: 'I am a trade unionist'. I express my regret that, for his own reason, that of resigning, he will no longer be speaking to us in this Chamber with the authority that he does now. I hope that he will have a long, fruitful and pleasant retirement."

After further compliments the Bishop spoke:

"My Lords, I do not often blush, but I am tempted to do so when I hear the very kind remarks from the Leader of the House, the Leader of the Opposition and the representative of the Liberal Party. I deeply appreciate the great kindness of your Lordships in speaking thus in this exceptional way. May I also say how much I have appreciated the forbearance and consideration of the House during the twenty-one years that I have tried to serve your Lordships . . .

"My Lords, during the last few weeks we have seen a stream of letters and have heard many speeches from Mr. Bulganin and Mr. Khrushchev advocating summit talks for the settlement of political differences and disarmament problems and for the promotion of world peace. I speak as one who desires that full advantage should be taken of these possibilities. But no Power which claims to be a champion of world peace and yet denies or undermines, and so attacks, religious liberty, is likely to convince other Powers which value that liberty of the genuineness of that championship while these attacks continue. There is an ominous development in the Eastern Zone of Germany to which I would call the attention of your Lordships. It is a sharpening in the last few months of that Government's campaign against religious liberty. The condition and fate of the Eastern Zone of Germany is a crucial factor in the international scene; its future is in many ways the key to the future of Germany; and the future of Germany, a peaceful and free Germany, is the key to the future of Europe . . .

"The East German Republic is a Socialist republic on the Marxist pattern. But the issue before us is not an economic issue, nor one of the shaping of an alternative political or social system. It is concerned solely with religious liberty, which, in theory, the East German Republic concedes . . .

"But practice and theory have not marched together. The Catholics, under their Bishop in Berlin and the Eastern Zone, Bishop Julius Doebfer, and the Protestants, under their Chief

Bishop, Bishop Otto Dibelius, both suffer. The majority of the Church people, the Christians in the Eastern Zone, are Protestants, and I naturally have a much greater knowledge of the Protestant Church than I have of the Catholic Church. But there has been in these years from time to time since the Constitution was adopted an anti-Church drive . . . Because of the Church's anxiety, on two occasions, guarantees, so far as the Protestants were concerned, were renewed at official conferences, with detailed protocols, the first being on 10th June, 1953, and the second on 3rd December, 1956. Each time the whole Zonal Cabinet, under Premier Grotewöhl on the one side and the East German Evangelical Church Leaders Conference, under Bishop Otto Dibelius, on the other side, endorsed and subscribed to these agreements. But experience has proved, as with the National Socialists, the inevitable logic of the totalitarian system which leads to the victory of the extremists.

"What are the facts? I put before your Lordships some of the recent developments hostile to religious liberty in two broad areas: first administrative, and, second, youth. As your Lordships have heard, the State guarantees the right of the Church to administer its affairs independently of the State. This should include a reasonable freedom of movement. In fact, there have been increasing restrictions on the movements of Church leaders, and ever since March, 1957, Bishop Otto Dibelius, President of the Evangelical Church for the whole of Germany, and Bishop of Berlin and Brandenburg, has been refused permission to enter the larger part of his diocese in the Eastern Zone. In his absence, the State-controlled Press has been filled with libels against him and against Church leaders generally.

"But it is not only restrictions of the clergy; the laity are restricted as well. For several years now there has been an annual rally of Evangelical churchmen known as the *Kirchentag,* numbering many hundreds of thousands. Last year it was planned to hold this *Kirchentag* in the Eastern Zone of Erfurt. Church people from all parts of Germany would have come, and a quarter of a million of those would have come from the Eastern Zone. After long negotiations with the government for permission, the plan was cancelled. The Minister of the Interior of the East German Government, Karl Meron, would consent to the holding of this *Kirchentag* at Erfurt only subject to the following conditions: first, that during the *Kirchentag,* everything should be avoided which would be likely to be considered as an endorsement of NATO policy and as 'being directed against peace'; second, that an official statement should be put out by the Praesidium, according to which the Praesidium would denounce all such events of the last *Kirchentag* at Frankfurt-am-Main in 1956, as in the view of the Government of the Soviet Occupied Zone it

'had constituted a criticism, by the official delegates, of the Soviet Zone's Government';

and third, that the Praesidium should give an assurance that representatives of the Government of the Soviet Zone belonging to the Protestant Church were to be given an opportunity, within the framework of the *Kirchentag*, to give an outline of the 'peace policy' of the Soviet Zone's Government.

"There is, I need not say, no truth at all in the suggestion that the Evangelical Church or the Catholic Church is a political establishment or a part of the North Atlantic Treaty Organisation. How ironical, however, that the East German Government should wish to take the opportunity of an immense Church rally from East and West Germany to do propaganda for the Soviet policy of 'world peace'! It is not surprising that such intolerable conditions were rejected.

"Other instances in this field, briefly, are these. There has been a drastic cancellation of licences to rebuild or repair churches, parish halls and vicarages, in spite of finance and raw materials being available during the last few months. Again, there has been the refusal of facilities for pastoral care at the All-German Church Synod in March, 1957. In Berlin, Bishop Jacobi revealed the considerable difficulties encountered in State institutions, prisons for juvenile delinquents and hospitals. At the Stalinstadt Hospital last Christmas, it was forbidden to read prayers with the sick. There have also been attacks increasingly on the Church welfare organisations, such as railway missions *Hilfswerke*, and again there has been a threat to Church finances.

"My second sphere is the most significant sphere of hostility – that is, the department of youth. Article 43 of the Constitution guarantees the right of the Church to organise religious instruction in State schools and school premises. In practice, recently in all State schools such instruction has been abolished on the plea of lack of accommodation. Article 42 guarantees that:

'No person shall be compelled to undergo religious instruction, to celebrate religious rites, or swear an oath in any religious form.'

"Article 48 guarantees:

'The right of parents to decide on their children's religious affiliation up to the age of fifteen years.'

"In fact a new pseudo-religious rite is, with all the power of the State, being imposed upon the young. It is called the *Jugendweihe*, or dedication of youth. It is definitely antagonistic to, and competing with, the Catholic and Protestant rite of Confirmation.

"A marked sign of the increasing hostility of the State for religious liberty appeared when, on 29th September last, Mr. Ulbricht, head of the Central Committee of the Communist Unity Party, laid down this directive:

'All young Germans will have to undergo a Communist youth dedication from 1958 onwards.'

"This *Jugendweihe* dedication is preceded by several months of cultural instruction from the age of thirteen. It is accompanied by very great pressure on the children and their parents to dissociate the children and the young from Church catechists and from Confirmation classes. In outward form and shape it is a rite which anticipates Christian Confirmation, but in content it stresses the factor of collective response and collective mass surrender.

"I should like to quote the three questions which are put to what are known as the dedicants, the youths who come forward *en masse*. The preceptor asks the whole mass:

'Are you ready to fight with all your strength, together with all patriots, for a united and independent Germany?
'Are you ready to fight with all your strength for World Peace and to defend it to the uttermost?
'Are you ready to fight with all your strength for the construction of a better and happier life on earth, for the progress in science, arts and economics?'

"To each question the host of these young initiates reply:

'Yes, we promise so to do.'

"Then the preceptor says:

'We have heard your solemn vow. Hence now receive the Great Promise of the community of all the workers united in the Workers' World Union, to protect you and to help you reach the high purpose to which you are now dedicated. Go forward fighting the good fight toward the vision of victory given to all honest working people on the earth.'

"This, my Lords is much more than a civic ceremony. It is intended to rule out the Christian rite. Bishop Dibelius, in Lent, 1956, said:

'The youth dedication rite is clearly and unmistakably based on the philosophy of dialectical materialism.'

"One has to choose which; it is a case of either this or the other. Some parents and young people may desire it. But to impose it on all is a grave contradiction of the guarantees of religious liberty.

"The intensity of the pressure applied is seen by the fact that in 1956 about three to four per cent or, say, six per cent of children of an age to receive Confirmation underwent the dedication rite. In 1957, the figure rose to between seven and ten per cent. But in 1958, according to Mr. Ulbricht's order, it is to be compulsory for 100 per cent. Certainly this makes religious liberty of no account. We have a record of the attacks on the leaders, ministers of the Church, and of the punishment inflicted by the State, which tells its own tale. During the last three months of 1957 alone, no fewer than sixty clergy and catechists were attacked by name in the Eastern Press. During the same period five pastors, two theological students and one catechist were sentenced to terms of imprisonment or penal servitude on charges of assaulting Confirmation pupils, currency smuggling or merely maintaining contact with Evangelical academics in West Germany.

"I ask your Lordships to picture the difficulty confronting Catholics and Protestants alike. They may be willing to accept the Communist Socialist State as a reality but this is very different from affirming their wholehearted allegiance to a totalitarian system. The difficulty in which they find themselves is fairly and clearly put in the following statement issued a fortnight ago, on 13th January, by the East German Evangelical Church Leaders' Conference – I quote:

'A Christian may duly find himself in a position to interpret the basis of his Christian faith in a direction towards affirming the economic and political contents of Socialism' – (Communist Socialism).

'What he cannot agree with, however, is a deliberate confusion of the economic and political expedients with the principles of an aggressively atheist and materialistic world concept.'

'The development in all other Peoples' Democracies of Eastern Europe demonstrates the possibility of being a loyal citizen in a socialist State without swearing a religious oath such as we have in our East Zone Republic, this Republic being the only Eastern State whose government officially sponsors the Communist youth dedication rite by limiting promotion to the dedicants exclusively and under-privileging the adherents of the Christian faith.'

"My Lords, this is a melancholy and, you may well think, discouraging tale, but it is one that it is necessary to tell. The Catholics and Protestants are at one in this. My purpose is to bring these facts before your Lordships as a very important part of the truth about the Eastern Zone of Germany. I have had some experience of the crushing of religious liberty in Germany by Hitler and the Nazis. Today, 30th January, is exactly the twenty-fifth anniversary of the appointment of Adolf Hitler as Chancellor. Some of the most conspicuous champions of religious liberty then find themselves in the same role today – notably Bishop Otto Dibelius. Men may look at the world and the human situation from different points of view, and they are entitled to different and opposing ideologies. No one should make a totalitarian claim for his own. But religious liberty is fundamental to civilised life. With all my heart I desire an understanding between the Western democracies and the Soviet Powers, but if the East German Zone as now administered is really proclaimed by the Moscow rulers to be a model State, the prospects of such a sincere understanding are hardly encouraging."[11]

The speech was listened to with rapt attention and respect.

Resignation of the Bishop

George Bell announced his resignation to his Diocesan Council on 4th June 1957. It was to take effect in about six months' time when he would be 74 years old. That was one year short of the required retirement age for a bishop. He surprised the Archbishop of Canterbury (Geoffrey Fisher), but he had good reasons for not waiting the extra year. A Lambeth Conference was due in 1958 and Chichester needed a new bishop to attend and carry through its recommendations. Jasper quotes a whole list of complimentary speeches made during a long series of farewell gatherings, many containing the sentiment of a friend: "He was the most humbly obstinate man I have ever known".

He had less than a year in retirement, but he crowded those remaining months of his life with a deep concern for human rights and above all, the unity of the Church. A holiday in Greece included conversations with Church leaders. In March he flew to Rome and visited many leading figures in the Vatican and had a special audience with the Pope. In April, he moved to Canterbury and with Mrs. Bell set up home in the Cathedral precincts. He remained co-chairman of the Anglican-Methodist conversations and was still in that office when the Lambeth Conference was held in July. After that he was in Denmark for the Central Committee of the World Council of Churches. When in Canterbury, he carefully arranged his papers in dated boxes in preparation for writing his memoirs. When I looked through these boxes after his death I realised how much he had helped his future biographers.

He died on Friday, 3rd October, 1958.

After his death, there were many tributes – especially from Germany. The most significant came in a long section of the definitive work, *The Churches and the Third Reich*, Volume Two, by Klaus Scholder.

Klaus Scholder was Professor of Modern Church History in Tübingen and Vice-Chairman of the German Evangelical Church's Commission for Contemporary History. He undertook to research the whole history of the Churches in the Third Reich. He lived only to complete the first two volumes, taking the story up to 1934. His research however covered the whole period of the Third Reich and others will complete the writing of further volumes. Already in his second volume he devotes a considerable section to Bell's influence and analyses it. His assessment of Bell is unequivocal:

> "While the struggle for the church in the Third Reich was thus coming to a new and largely visible climax, the resolve to help the oppressed Christians in Germany was also growing in Protestant churches abroad.

"One focal point of these concerns was in London. There lived and worked one of the most significant ecclesiastical figures of the first half of our century, the Bishop of Chichester, G. K. A. Bell . . . Whereas for most English people the theological traditions of the continent were remote, Bell had a sure feel for the basic positions in the German church struggle. From summer 1933 on he followed the Confessing Church indefatigably and without a moment's hesitation or uncertainty, and even during the war, when everything seemed to sink into a flood of hatred, he remained the unshakeable friend of the other Germany, of whose existence and credibility he tried in vain to convince the Foreign Office."[12]

Notes

1. *Die Evangelische Kirche nach dem Zusammenbruch*, Vandenhoeck & Ruprecht, Göttingen, 1988. (A Collection of documents, mostly in English, of reports by foreign observers of Germany in 1945.) Edited by Clemens Vollnhals. Complete text of Bell's report of the October 1945 visit, pp. 224–233. The quote is from the last paragraph, p. 233.
2. *Ibid.* Complete text of report of the British Council of Churches Delegation, pp. 286–296. The quote is from p. 288.
3. *Ibid.* Complete text of Cotter's report to the Control Commission of the visit of the British Churches Delegation, pp. 266–286. The quote is from pp. 274–275.
4. *Ibid.*, p. 277.
5. Werner Hühne, *A Man to be Reckoned with*, SCM Press, London, 1962, p. 80.
6. *Die Evangelische Kirche nach dem Zusammenbruch*, pp. 255–256.
7. *Kirchliche Zeitgeschichte*, p. 13 (edited). The complete German text, pp. 210–220 (Die Situation der Kirchen in der sowjetischen Besatzungszone).
8. Jasper, *op. cit.*, pp. 311–312.
9. Johannes Hamel, *A Christian in East Germany*, SCM Press, London, 1960, pp. 15–17.
10. Richard W. Solberg, *God and Caesar in East Germany*, Macmillan, New York, 1961, pp. 287–288.
11. *Hansard*, House of Lords, 30th January 1958.
12. Klaus Scholder, *op. cit.*, Vol. II, p. 75.

12 George Bell's Relevance for the 'Nineties

An Anglican Bishop, whose perception of Anglo-German relations in the 'thirties, 'forties and 'fifties was crucial for our understanding of Europe then, may appear to be irrelevant to the totally changed situation of the 'nineties. The only justification we might have for making a careful study of his insights is that he grappled with the problems that we see beginning to reappear in a reunited Germany and hopefully a single Europe.

There are at least three areas in which the experiences and insights of George Bell are of relevance still and there may yet be others.

The first is in his understanding of the German *psyche*. Over a period of thirty years he was consistently right when many around him were mistaken. He recognised at an early stage the compelling influence of the *völkisch* element in the German character. The word is difficult to translate but I have tried to explain its meaning in the course of this book. It is not racist although it can provide the basis for an ugly theory of racism. It is a sense of being a people, rather than a nation. History has contributed to it – the conquest of the Roman Empire, the cultural links between divided states with a common language over a long period, the inability to build an empire, the humiliation of defeat and with it a sense of inferiority. All this Bell saw and, through three stages, explained what was happening among the German people. In the rise of Nazism, he saw an assertion of a culture which wished to be proud after humiliation. During the rule of Nazism he saw that the Nazis were not seeking territory except as a symbol of their cultural pride. In the defeat of Germany, he saw a people in need of assurance.

In the first of these stages, he urged an understanding of what we had done with the humiliating terms of the Versailles Treaty. In the second he pleaded with statesmen to negotiate with the Germans in terms of human rights, not simply territorial concessions. In the third he worked for the acceptance of Germany within the concourse of nations. His approach to Germany at all three stages was to converse with Germans about human rights and national dignity. His keen desire for peace may have been ideological but he saw peaceful discussion with Germans as the only way to solve problems which would otherwise destroy European civilisation.

Bell is still relevant in his diagnosis of the effects upon a proud nation of the humiliation of defeat. He recognised that when a war is undertaken for the best of reasons, the ultimate victory must be followed by a just peace or it will lead to further war. The years since 1945 have provided ample examples of failures to understand this and, at the time of writing, it is obvious that the lessons of Versailles should be learned in connection with the Serbian expansions.

The second area in which George Bell is relevant still is the consistent belief in the unity of Europe. He believed this unity to be based upon Christian foundations. His resistance to what he called "The aggressive and imperialistic Bolshevik and Nazi regimes" was based upon his observation that they were "the enemies of a transcendental religion, and that both persecute the Christian Church". From the beginning of his public life until the end, this was the heart of his message. But he interpreted it – not as defending the Church – but as caring for the victims of aggression. His humanitarian work for refugees from Hitler's Germany, honoured by Jews and Christians alike, as well as humanists, was based upon the conviction that human values are only safe with a religious foundation. For that reason he supported the resistance of the Christian Church in Germany and his last protest was against the denial of religious liberty in the Soviet Zone of East Germany. A denial of the faith which built a united Europe leads to its disintegration. This led him to believe and act upon the truth that "the fundamental thing is the human factor". No system however good will work unless this is taken care of. The unity of Europe depends upon the Judaeo-Christian view of human rights.

The third area where George Bell continues to be relevant is in his consistent support of movements towards unity within the Church. This was no minor issue for him, no question of tidy organisation, no economic solution of the perilous finances of the Christian Church in many lands. Unity for Bell was the precondition of effectiveness. The Church failed at every point because it was weakened by division. The mobilising of the spiritual resources of a United Church, he believed, would be enough to assure human rights, prevent war and allow the Kingdom of God to shine upon the world, and he would retain that belief still.

The events that followed his death in 1958 would have concerned him deeply had he lived. He would have rejoiced at the fall of the Berlin Wall and all it symbolised, but I imagine that he would be warning us against triumphalism. The problems were just beginning in 1989 and he would have seen that. The former communist states needed more than the end of communism to solve their problems. He saw the danger of disunity between the Catholic West and the Orthodox East and how important it would be to mobilise the resources of the Orthodox Churches for the healing of the post-Communist East. He would have seen the dangers inherent in a reunited Germany, but at the same time cautioned against fears of its rising power. He would be arguing for support for the former territories of the Soviet Union, because it is in our own interest to strengthen the movement that makes for openness and religious freedom. He would be with those who saw the necessity of the union of the churches for the sake of humankind.

He was not always listened to in his own day and the consequences were evident in the near destruction of Europe. His story can help us face the value of a reunited Germany, the necessity for one Europe including Eastern Europe and the urgent desire of God that his Church should be One.

His vision is clearly seen in the lines of his hymn:

"Let love's unconquerable might
Your scattered companies unite
In service to the Lord of Light;
So shall God's will on earth be done,
New lamps be lit, new tasks begun,
And the whole Church at last be one."

The Failure of Theology

But perhaps the greatest contribution of George Bell was his clear assessment of where and how the theology of the churches of Europe failed them in the time of testing. He was in a unique position to see the development of theology in Germany and the failure, even of Karl Barth, to grasp the dimension of evil with which the churches had to deal. His closeness to the Scandinavian churches and his central position in the ecumenical movement enabled him to see the failure of that movement to develop a theology which was competent to relate to the issues of the contemporary world. He had the gift of learning from others and, although not himself an original theologian, he could see the penetrating insights of men like Adolf Deismann, Nathan Söderblom, Otto Dibelius, and more directly of Dietrich Bonhoeffer. He learned also from Gerhard Leibholz, who although not an academic theologian was a distinguished international lawyer with a grasp of theology. He not only learned from the insights of others, but could often apply them to the real world more effectively than these original thinkers could themselves. He was a catalyst whose writings and speeches can still give meaning to our modern world in peace and war.

BIBLIOGRAPHY

H. N. Bate (ed)	*Faith & Order: Lausanne 1927*, SCM Press, London, 1927.
G. K. A. Bell	*A Brief Sketch of the Church of England*, SCM Press, London, 1929.
G. K. A. Bell	*Christianity and World Order*, Penguin Books, London, 1940.
G. K. A. Bell (ed)	*Documents on Christian Unity 1920–24*, OUP, London, 1924.
G. K. A. Bell	<u>in</u> *Evangelisches Archivzentral*, Berlin.
G. K. A. Bell	*Humanity and the Refugees*, University College, London, 1939.
G. K. A. Bell & Adolf Deissmann (edd)	*Mysterium Christi*, Longmans, Green & Co., London, 1930.
G. K. A. Bell	*The Bell Papers* in Lambeth Palace Library.
G. K. A. Bell	*The Church and Humanity*, Longmans, Green & Co., London, 1946.
G. K. A. Bell	*The Kingship of Christ*, Penguin Books, London, 1954.
G. K. A. Bell	*The Stockholm Conference 1925*, OUP, London, 1926.
Gerhard Besier (ed)	*Kirchliche Zeitgeschichte*, Göttingen and Berlin, 1988 onwards.
Gerhard Besier	*"Selbstreinigung" unter britischer Besatzungherrschaft*, Vandenhoeck & Ruprecht, 1986.
Eberhard Bethge & Ronald Jasper (edd)	*An der Schwelle zum Gespaltenen Europa*, Kreuz Verlag, Stuttgart and Berlin, 1974.
Eberhard Bethge	*Dietrich Bonhoeffer*, E. T. Collins, London, 1967.
Marc Boegner	*The Long Road to Unity*, Collins, London, 1970.
Dietrich Bonhoeffer	*Predigen, Auslegungen, Meditationen*, Band 2, 1935–1945, Chr. Kaiser Verlag, München, 1985.

Dietrich Bonhoeffer	*The Cost of Discipleship*, SCM Press, London, 1959.
Andrew Chandler	*A Question of 'Fundamental Principles': The Church of England and the Persecution of the Jews in Germany 1933–37* in Leo Baeck Institute Yearbook 1993.
Andrew Chandler	*The Church of England and National Socialist Germany 1933–1945*, unpublished Ph.D. thesis available in Cambridge University Library.
Andrew Chandler	*The Death of Dietrich Bonhoeffer* in Journal of Ecclesiastical History 1994.
Adolf Deissmann	*Light from the Ancient East*, 4th Edition, Harper & Brothers, New York and London, 1922.
F. T. Grossmith	*The Cross and the Swastika*, H. E. Walter, Worthing, 1984.
Johannes Hamel	*A Christian in East Germany*, SCM Press, London, 1960.
Adrian Hastings	*A History of English Christianity 1920–1985*, Collins, London, 1986.
Werner Hühne	*A Man to be Reckoned With*, SCM Press, London, 1962.
Ronald C. D. Jasper	*George Bell: Bishop of Chichester*, OUP, London, 1967.
Sabine Leibholz-Bonhoeffer	*The Bonhoeffers: Portrait of a Family*, Covenant Publications, Chicago, 1994.
Oxford Scholars' Conference	*Remembering for the Future*, Pergamon Press, Oxford and New York, 1988.
William Paton	*The Church and the New Order*, SCM Press, London, 1941.
Edwin Robertson	*Christians Against Hitler*, SCM Press, London, 1962.
Edwin Robertson (ed)	*No Rusty Swords*, Collins, London, 1965.
Edwin Robertson (ed & tr)	*The Pastor of Buchenwald*, SCM Press, London, 1955.

Edwin Robertson	*The Shame and the Sacrifice*, Hodder and Stoughton, London, 1987.
Edwin Robertson (ed)	*True Patriotism*, Collins, London, 1973.
Gordon Rupp	*I Seek my Brethren*, Epworth, London, 1975.
Klaus Scholder	*Requiem for Hitler*, SCM Press, London, 1989.
Klaus Scholder	*The Churches and the Third Reich*, Vol. I, SCM Press, London, 1987, Vol. II, SCM Press, London, 1988.
Kenneth Slack	*George Bell*, SCM Press, London, 1971.
Richard W. Solberg	*God and Caesar in East Germany*, Macmillan, New York, 1961.
William Stählin	*Via Vitae: Lebenserinnerungen*, Kassel, 1966.
Ger Van Roon	*German Resistance to Hitler*, Van Nostrand Reinhold Co. Ltd., New York, 1971.
Maurice Villain	*Unity*, Harvill Press, London, 1963.
W. A. Visser 't Hooft	*The First Assembly of the World Council of Churches: The Official Report*, SCM Press, London, 1949.
Clemens Vollnhals (ed)	*Die Evangelische Kirche nach dem Zusammenbruch*, Vandenhoeck & Ruprecht, Göttingen, 1988.

INDEX

Adenauer, Konrad 137
Alexander, Viscount 149–50
Althaus, Paul, 13–15, 21
Ammundsen, V. 34, 38
Archibald, General 145
Asmussen, Hans 110, 125
Attlee, Clement 107–8
Aubrey, M. E. 106, 122–3, 139
Augustine, St 56

Bach, J. S. 145
Baillie, John 139
Balfour, Michael 94–5
Barth, Karl 2, 9, 14, 22, 35, 38,
    119, 120, 122, 126, 160
Bate, H. N. 23
Beattie, Major 118–9
Belgion, Montgomery 131
Bell, Henrietta 64, 156
Bell, James 1
Bentwich, Norman 48
Berggrav, Eivind 4, 84, 86,
    94, 133
Bertram, Cardinal 117
Besier, Gerhard iv, 118, 127
Bethge, Eberhard 24, 36, 45,
    62, 73
Bevin, Ernest 108
Bickersteth, Samuel 1
Bismarck 75
Boeckheler, Pastor 63
Boegner, Marc 105, 115, 131–2,
    136, 138
Bonhoeffer, Dietrich 2–3, 24–31,
    34–39, 42–3, 45, 52, 62–3, 65,
    68–70, 72–3, 81, 83–5, 87, 89,
    96–7, 102, 104, 109, 112, 160
Bormann, Martin 130
Bourne, Cardinal 42
Braley, E. F. 23

Brilioth, Y. T. 86
Bulganin, N. 150

Churchill, Winston 78–9, 85, 88,
    90, 107
Clay, General 124–5
Clutton Brock, Guy 107
Coffin, H. S. 70
Collins, Kenneth E. 60
Cooper, Duff 78
Cotter, Arthur 116, 140–1, 157
Courvoisier, Professor 136
Cripps, Stafford 84
Crossett, Bob 126
Crossman, Richard 91
Curtis, Lionel 93

Daladier, President 57
Darnley, Earl of 76
Davidson, Randall 1–2, 11, 17,
    21, 80, 136
Deedes, William 107
Deissmann, Adolf 2–10, 15–16,
    18, 22, 39, 160
Dibelius, Otto 22, 106, 109–10,
    140–1, 144, 150–1, 154–5, 160
Dodd, C. H. 10
Doebfer, Julius 150
Dolfuss, Engelbert 37
Donnitz, Admiral 137
Downey, Richard 47
Duncan-Jones, A. S. 21

Eden, Anthony 82, 84–5, 88–9,
    97
Ehrenstrom, Nils 86
Eidem, Erling 29, 85
Eliot, T. S. 1, 85

165